RULES FOR RESISTANCE

RULES FOR RESISTANCE

Advice from Around the Globe for the Age of Trump

With an introduction by David Cole

Edited by Melanie Wachtell Stinnett and David Cole

THE NEW PRESS
25 YEARS

NEW YORK
LONDON

Requests for permission to reproduce selections from this
book should be mailed to: Permissions Department,
The New Press, 120 Wall Street, 31st floor, New York, NY 10005.

Published in the United States by The New Press, New York, 2017
Distributed by Perseus Distribution

ISBN 978-1-62097-354-7 (pb)
ISBN 978-1-62097-355-4 (e-book)
CIP data is available

The New Press publishes books that promote and enrich public discussion and
understanding of the issues vital to our democracy and to a more equitable world.
These books are made possible by the enthusiasm of our readers; the support
of a committed group of donors, large and small; the collaboration of our many
partners in the independent media and the not-for-profit sector; booksellers,
who often hand-sell New Press books; librarians; and above all by our authors.

www.thenewpress.com

Composition by dix!

Printed in the United States of America

2   4   6   8   10   9   7   5   3   1

CONTENTS

INTRODUCTION

I suspect that for most Americans, *It Can't Happen Here,* Sinclair Lewis's satirical novel about the rise of a populist president who defeats Franklin Delano Roosevelt and imposes authoritarian rule, has always been a comforting title. Lewis intended the book and its title to be a warning to the complacent. But complacent we have largely been. Novels like Lewis's, and Philip Roth's *The Plot Against America*, are just that, novels. Alternative histories. Thought experiments. Surely it can't happen here.

These days, the alternative histories seem somehow less satirical and more prescient. The election of Donald J. Trump took most Americans, most of the world, and indeed Trump himself by surprise. He hardly earned a mandate, winning through the peculiarities of the Electoral College despite losing the popular vote. If we elected presidents the way we elect every other federal official, by majority vote, Hillary Clinton would be president. But despite earning the White House without even a majority of the voters supporting him, President Trump has proceeded to surround himself with advisers and cabinet secretaries who are, by and large, long on conspiracy theories and right-wing ideology, short on relevant experience, competence, and judgment, and dismissive of basic values of the rule of law.

As a candidate, Donald Trump threatened to ban Muslims, build a wall on the Mexican border, jail his opponent, "open up" the libel laws, repeal the Affordable Care Act, revive waterboarding, and overturn *Roe v. Wade.* As a president-elect, he tweeted that those who dared to burn an American flag should be imprisoned and stripped of their U.S. citizenship, both blatantly unconstitutional proposals. As president, he has not moderated his approach. He has ignored a constitutional prohibition on conflicts of interest, maintaining full ownership of his private businesses even as he assumes the office of the presidency. He has appointed officials to run agencies that they would just as soon eliminate, excluded his critics from press briefings, imposed gag rules on government employees, and improperly contacted the FBI over an investigation of Trump's campaign aides' contacts with Russia while Russian agents were hacking Democratic emails to boost Trump's chances.

He has ordered a massive increase in deportations and announced plans to begin construction of a wall on the Mexican border. He issued an executive order that for the first time in our history introduced a religious litmus test into our immigration policy. It barred all entry from seven Muslim-majority countries and gave a preference to refugees from "minority" faiths that he explained on national television was designed to favor Christians. The executive order was condemned by the presidents of every major university, by the leading science organizations, by refugee and human rights groups, and even by former vice president Dick Cheney, former CIA director Michael Hayden, and former Justice Department lawyer John Yoo, the man who wrote the memoranda that authorized torture in the Bush administration. It is no exaggeration to say that never before in this country's history have our fundamental values been more deeply threatened by the occupant of the Oval Office.

The essays collected here come from across the world, from countries that have seen the rise of autocratic power in a wide variety of political settings and systems. None of the authors here can say, "It can't happen here." They have lived through strongman regimes, repression of critics, and populist appeals to xenophobia and division. Reading them provides a sobering reminder that democracy, basic civil rights, and the rule of law are neither inevitable nor self-executing. The separation of powers, a charter of rights, and a written constitution are no guarantee. They must be actively defended from those who would thrust them aside in the name of populism or security.

At the same time, these essays provide critical guidance on how to resist the abuses that Trump threatens. One theme in particular unites virtually all the contributors: whether one faces an autocrat in Turkey, Russia, Chile, the Philippines, Egypt, Italy, Venezuela— or the United States—the principal defense lies in the institutions of civil society—or more directly, in an engaged citizenry. It is no accident that tyrants so often target the media, the academy, religion, and nongovernmental organizations: these are the sources of independent authority, citizen mobilization, critique, and resistance. It is also no accident that repressive regimes take aim at freedom of speech and association. Throughout the world, it is these rights and institutions that have the potential to check the abuse of power.

In just its first weeks, the Trump administration has displayed a disturbing willingness to attack our democratic institutions, in particular the independent press. Trump has called the news media the "enemy of the people" and has dismissed as "fake news" mainstream journalism that reflects unfavorably on his own self-image, even as he is silent with respect to actual lies presented as "news" by his supporters. He has lamented leaks to the press and threatened a crackdown on leakers. This behavior echoes the treatment of the press both in authoritarian regimes across the globe and in democracies where autocratic leaders have assumed power. Several of the essays collected here come from journalists who have labored under such conditions, and much worse. They offer important lessons for the media, whose legitimacy turns on a degree of objectivity and fidelity to the truth, and who, because of that ideal, perform a critical checking function even as they incur the wrath of leaders who prefer not to be questioned or criticized.

In the United States, civil society remains vibrant. Thus far, the press has not been cowed by President Trump, and subscriptions to newspapers like the *New York Times* and *Washington Post* have soared. Nongovernmental organizations like my own, the American Civil Liberties Union, have stood up to Trump, and attracted unprecedented and widespread popular support in doing so. Universities, and the students and professors who study there, have been unsparing in their critiques. Religious communities have been at the forefront of many protests. And ordinary citizens have come out like never before in defense of basic values and liberties. The women's marches across the country (and world) the day after Trump's inauguration were only the first salvo. Airport protests of the Muslim ban, demonstrations at the White House and Trump Tower, town halls that have called out our congressional representatives for their failure to stand up to Trump, are all signs of a healthy democracy, in which the citizenry maintains a strong fidelity to the values that Trump threatens to dismantle.

Citizens concerned about Trump eagerly want to know what they can do. *The Indivisible Guide*, published in book form here for the first time, provides important and timely answers. It was written by former congressional staffers to educate citizens on how to influence their elected representatives. It is a guide on how to become a citizen activist. More than a million people have downloaded the guide, and *Indivisible* groups have sprung up in every congressional district across the country. In part inspired by the guide and the activism it spurred, people showed up in droves at town halls held by politicians of all political stripes during Congress's first break of 2017. The guide and the movement it has helped inspire offer an extraordinary example of how American citizens can mobilize to resist antidemocratic impulses from our government. It is precisely in this type of civic engagement that our salvation lies.

As the essays in this volume also remind us, however, if we as citizens do not mobilize, do not remain vigilant, do not continue to stand up for what we believe in, the road to repression is all too open. It can happen here. The only thing that will stop it from doing so is a citizenry that understands both the gravity of the threat *and* the power of an organized, popular resistance. The institutions of democracy are only as strong as our willingness to stand and fight for them. As Learned Hand, a great federal court of appeals judge, once wrote: "Liberty lies in the hearts of men and women; when it dies there, no constitution, no law, no court can save it; no constitution, no law, no court can even do much to help it." Bearing witness from around the world, from the Fourth Estate, and from the halls of Congress, the authors collected here underscore the truth of Learned Hand's warning. The ultimate defense of liberty lies in us.

—David Cole
March 2017

RULES FOR RESISTANCE

Part I

Europe

I WATCHED A POPULIST LEADER RISE IN MY COUNTRY. THAT'S WHY I'M GENUINELY WORRIED FOR AMERICA

Miklós Haraszti

(Hungary)

Originally published in *The Washington Post* (December 28, 2016)

Hungary, my country, has in the past half decade morphed from an exemplary post–Cold War democracy into a populist autocracy. Here are a few eerie parallels that have made it easy for Hungarians to put Donald Trump on their political map: Prime Minister Viktor Orban has depicted migrants as rapists, job stealers, terrorists, and "poison" for the nation, and built a vast fence along Hungary's southern border. The popularity of his nativist agitation has allowed him to easily debunk as unpatriotic or partisan any resistance to his self-styled "illiberal democracy," which he said he modeled after "successful states" such as Russia and Turkey.

No wonder Orban feted Trump's victory as ending the era of "liberal nondemocracy," "the dictatorship of political correctness," and "democracy export." The two consummated their political kinship in a recent phone conversation; Orban is invited to Washington, where, they agreed, both had been treated as "black sheep."

When friends encouraged me to share my views on the US election, they may have looked for heartening insights from a member of the European generation that managed a successful transition from communist autocracy to liberal constitutionalism. Alas, right now I find it hard to squeeze hope from our past experiences, because halting elected post-truthers in countries split by partisan fighting is much more difficult than achieving freedom where it is desired by virtually everyone.

But based on our current humiliating condition, I may observe what governing style to expect from the incoming populist in chief and what fallacies should be avoided in countering his ravages.

A first vital lesson from my Hungarian experience: Do not be distracted by a delusion of impending normalization. Do not ascribe a rectifying force to statutes, logic, necessities, or fiascoes. Remember the frequently reset and always failed illusions attached to an eventual normalization of Vladimir Putin, Recep Tayyip Erdoğan, and Orban.

Call me a typical Hungarian pessimist, but I think hope can be damaging when dealing with populists. For instance, hoping that unprincipled populism is unable to govern. Hoping that Trumpism is self-deceiving, or self-revealing, or self-defeating. Hoping to find out if the president-elect will have a line or a core, or if he is driven by beliefs or by interests. Or there's the Kremlinology-type hope that Trump's party, swept to out-and-out power by his charms, could turn against him. Or hope extracted, oddly, from the very fact that he often disavows his previous commitments.

Populists govern by swapping issues, as opposed to resolving them. Purposeful randomness, constant ambush, relentless slaloming, and red herrings dropped all around are the new normal. Their favorite means of communication is provoking conflict. They do not mind being hated. Their two basic postures of "defending" and "triumphing" are impossible to perform without picking enemies.

I was terrified to learn that pundits in the United States have started to elaborate on possible benefits of Trump's stances toward Russia and China. Few developments are more frightening than the populist edition of George Orwell's dystopia. The world is now dominated by three gigantic powers, Oceania, Eurasia, and Eastasia, aka the United States, Russia, and China, respectively, and all three are governed by promises of making their realms "great again."

Please do not forget that populists can turn into peaceniks or imperialists at any moment, depending on what they think could yield good spin that boosts their support. Remember how Putin and Erdoğan had switched, within months this year, from warring to fraternity. Or how Orban in opposition had blasted any compromises with Russia, only to become Putin's best friend upon his election.

I have plenty of gloomy don't-dos but few proven trump cards. There is perhaps one mighty exception, the issue of corruption, which the polite American media like to describe as "conflicts of interest."

It is the public's moral indignation over nepotism that has proved to be the nemesis of illiberal regimes. Personal and family greed, cronyism, thievery combined with hypocrisy are in the genes of illiberal autocracy, and in many countries betrayed expectations of a selfless strongman have led to a civic awakening.

It probably helps to be as watchful as possible on corruption, to assist investigative journalism at any price, and to defend the institutions that enforce transparency and justice. And it also helps to have leaders in the opposition who not only are impeccably clean in pecuniary matters, but also impress as such.

The world is looking at the United States now in a way that we never thought would be possible: fretting that the "deals" of its new president will make the world's first democracy more similar to that of the others. I wish we onlookers could help the Americans in making the most out of their hard-to-change Constitution. We still are thankful for what they gave to the world, and we will be a bit envious if they can stop the fast-spreading plague of national populism.

ADVICE FROM EUROPE FOR ANTI-TRUMP PROTESTERS

Anne Applebaum
(Poland)

Originally published in *The Washington Post* (November 16, 2016)

Forgive me for what is going to sound like an odd analogy, but the street demonstrations across the United States have given me an uncanny sense of déjà vu.

I live part of the time in Warsaw, and I was there last year during an ugly election. Hateful screeds about Muslim immigrants (though there are hardly any Muslim immigrants in Poland) and angry "anti-elitist" rhetoric overwhelmed a stiff and unpopular female leader; the center-right and center-left politicians split into quarreling factions, allowing a radical populist party to win with a minority of voters. Upon taking power, it set out to destroy the country's democratic and state institutions: the constitutional court, the independent prosecutor, the independent civil service, the public media.

Poles took to the streets. There were huge demonstrations, the largest since the collapse of communism in 1989. Nobody had expected them, and—like the demonstrations in US cities last week—nobody had planned these marches in advance. A year later, here are some reflections on their value:

Protest makes people feel better.
Because the government's language was vicious and angry, the demonstrators tried hard to be nice and polite. During protest marches,

they didn't walk on the grass. They chanted for "freedom, equality, democracy," which has a nice lilt to it in Polish. The middle-aged ex-radicals who had demonstrated against communism in the 1980s felt energized and young again. The boost to morale was real. I am sure that's true for many marching in New York or San Francisco this week, too.

Protest, if not carefully targeted, achieves little.
The Polish protests were meant to "defend the constitution," a very theoretical goal. Because they were about a principle, not a policy, the government found them easy to ignore, and the slogans never inspired younger or rural voters. Sound familiar?

The calculus did shift, it is true, when hundreds of thousands of Polish women dressed in black joined a national protest against a very harsh proposed abortion law. The protest was aimed at a specific measure. It took place not just in Warsaw and Krakow, but also in every city in the country, as well as many smaller towns. Perhaps the sight of so many angry women spooked the party leader, Jaroslaw Kaczynski, who is an elderly bachelor; perhaps the thousands of photographs that appeared all over the world frightened the prime minister, who is female. In any case, this targeted, well-organized, broadly based single-issue protest had far more impact than the general marches, and the government withdrew the law.

Protests inspire conspiracy theorists.
Authoritarian personalities don't believe in spontaneity. They think that everything is part of a plot to deceive them. Trump's first tweet, as president-elect, referred to protesters as "paid." Similarly, Kaczynski has implied variously that protesters are former members of the Communist Party or secret police, that they are agents of foreign powers or, in the words of another radical politician, are in the pay of an unnamed "Jewish banker." This line of thinking allows the rulers to discount the protesters. If they are "paid" or "foreign" or "manipulated," after all, then they can be ignored. Also, the hard-core

voting base—in Poland, about 20 percent of the country—can be inspired to focus its hatred and anger on the "traitors" instead of listening to what they are trying to say.

Politics matter more than protests.

A year after the street movement began, its leaders, the "Committee to Defend Democracy," have become an important part of national political culture. Their marches and meetings inspire people. Their television appearances are carefully watched. But because they kept their distance from political parties, they haven't much altered opinion polls. The government is still supported by a committed minority. The center-right and the center-left remain splintered into smaller groups. If anything, the protest movement seems to have solidified a general disdain for politics and a dislike of politicians in general.

In a democracy, real change comes through politics, political parties, and elections.

Poland, although damaged, is still a democracy. If the people who are willing to put time into demonstrations also prove willing to work on behalf of candidates in local elections—or to become candidates themselves—they will achieve far more. A mayor is in a far better position to resist attacks on the civil service than a man carrying a sign. A different parliamentary majority could block the would-be authoritarian government altogether.

The same thing is true in the United States. Five Democratic senators could do more to block extremist judges or damaging policies than 5 million—or even 50 million—people chanting slogans. Protesting might make you feel better, it might win a few battles, and it might attract attention. I'm sorry if you are angry at "the establishment," but you need to work for it and within it if you want it to change.

DONALD TRUMP, AMERICA'S OWN SILVIO BERLUSCONI

Alexander Stille

(Italy)

Originally published in shorter form in *The Intercept*
(March 7, 2016)

As someone who has covered Silvio Berlusconi closely since his entrance into politics in 1993, it has been difficult not to be overcome with a powerful sense of déjà vu watching the presidential campaign of Donald Trump.

Some of the resemblances are obvious as well as uncanny. Both are billionaires who made their initial fortunes in real estate, whose wealth and playboy lifestyle turned them into celebrities. They are each masters of media manipulation and shaping of their own public image, Berlusconi as Italy's largest private mass media company owner, Trump as the star of his own reality TV show and creator of the Trump "brand." Both stunned their respective political establishments by winning national elections in unexpected ways, breaking most of the rules of traditional politics.

Entering politics, both have styled themselves as the ultimate antipolitician, as the rich, supersuccessful entrepreneur running against gray "professional politicians" who have never met a payroll and are ruining their respective countries. Both are deliberately transgressive, breaking through the tedium of politics as usual by insulting and shouting down opponents, using vulgar language, simple catchy slogans, off-color jokes, and misogynistic remarks.

These verbal "gaffes"—which would be suicide for most

politicians—are actually part of their appeal. I recall when Berlusconi presided over a European summit and when negotiations stalled he said to the assembled heads of state, "Let's lighten up the tone and talk about soccer and women. You, Gerhardt," he said, turning to Gerhard Schroeder, then chancellor of Germany, who has been married four times, "perhaps you can tell us about women." The remark was greeted with a chill. At first I thought, how could Berlusconi be so foolish, and then it occurred to me that I (or even the European heads of state) was not his audience. After all, what are the two favorite topics in most Italian bars? Soccer and women. Similarly, one might have thought that Trump might have doomed himself with remarks about TV journalist Megyn Kelly's menstrual cycle, and his ability to get "a young and beautiful piece of ass." But this common touch has allowed both Berlusconi and Trump to successfully create a very unusual hybrid persona: a kind of everyman's billionaire. Someone who, on the one hand, by virtue of his extreme wealth, success, and audacity is a kind of superman to whom the normal rules of conduct don't apply. At the same time, whose plain and even vulgar speech connects viscerally with ordinary people, particularly the less educated part of the electorate. This gives both of them a seemingly improbable interclass appeal, very rich men who pursue policies that benefit the very rich (see the proposed Trump tax cut) while making effective rhetorical appeals to the grievances of the struggling members of the middle and working classes.

Both Berlusconi and Trump are creatures of a postideological age, in which personality and entertainment values have replaced political parties and programs. Berlusconi entered politics after the fall of the Berlin Wall when the two major parties of the Cold War period, the Christian Democratic Party and the Italian Communist Party, were dissolved. Neither Trump nor Berlusconi has a real political program; what they are selling is themselves. Berlusconi used to say that what Italy needs is more Berlusconi (they both have a penchant for grandiosity and referring to themselves in the third person). I recall a very telling moment during Berlusconi's first election campaign: During a TV debate his opponent, the economist Luigi Spaventa, was pointing out the holes and inconsistencies in Berlusconi's economic program, Berlusconi stopped him in midsentence and pointed to the victories of his soccer club, AC Milan: "Before trying to compete with me, try, at least, winning a couple of national championships!" The remark had the air of unassailable truth—however irrelevant it might be to Berlusconi's fitness to govern. Similarly, when asked how he is going to get Mexico to pay for a giant wall between their country and ours, Trump simply responds, "Don't worry, they'll pay!" Like Berlusconi, Trump offers himself, not a program, as the solution: "I am your voice," he said memorably in his acceptance speech at the Republican National Convention. "No one knows the system better than me, which is why I alone can fix it."

But aside from these clear parallels, there is another element that links them that may explain why Italy and the United States are the two major democracies in which we have seen this phenomenon: the almost total deregulation of broadcast media. Berlusconi managed through political connections (with evidence of massive bribery) to acquire a virtual monopoly of private television in the 1970s. He introduced highly partisan news programs that bear more than a few resemblances to Fox News. (In the United States, radio and television became almost entirely deregulated during the Reagan administration in the 1980s.) He gave TV shows to on-air bullies like Vittorio Sgarbi and Paolo Liguori, who peddled conspiracy theories like Glenn Beck and shouted down and bullied political opponents in styles not unlike that of Bill O'Reilly.

It's important to recall that the transformation of the media landscape of both Italy and the United States did not simply happen, but was the result, in part, of political decisions. Although it seems like speaking about "covered wagons" and the pony express, only about thirty years ago, there were rules of the Federal Communications Commission (FCC) called the Fairness Doctrine and the Equal Time Doctrine. This was seen as a way of guaranteeing that the public interest and a certain degree of pluralism of views were respected when broadcast licenses were issued to private companies. These rules made a certain amount of sense in an age in which analog frequencies were limited in number. Television (and television news) was dominated by the big three networks, each of whom was competing for as much of the total market as it could get. In this setup, it made no sense to create an overtly partisan newscast that could alienate either Republican or Democratic viewers. This was hardly a golden age—broadcast news was arguably dull, centrist, and establishmentarian. But basic rules of civility and a certain respect for factual accuracy applied. News anchors like Walter Cronkite, who hosted the *CBS Evening News* from 1962 to 1981, were among the most respected men in America, and it may seem naïve today but they believed him when he ended each broadcast with the words "and that's the way it was."

With the advent of cable television in the 1970s and the Reagan revolution of the 1980s this all changed. Ronald Reagan's FCC commissioner Mark Fowler insisted that television was no different than any other commercial appliance, "a toaster with pictures," he called it.

The technological changes in the field—the emergence of cable—reinforced this position. With dozens and eventually hundreds of channels, it was felt, the old rules of fairness and balance were passé. The sheer number of channels would guarantee pluralism.

What this view failed to appreciate was that it didn't correspond with the way people actually consume news: They do not watch multiple points of view, switching frequently between PBS, Fox News, MSNBC, and CNN; instead each group seeks out the news that fits its own ideological assumptions and stays there.

In 1987, Fowler eliminated the Fairness Doctrine. The next year Rush Limbaugh created his nationally syndicated radio program. Fox News began operating in 1995. With deregulation and cable an entirely new business model was formed: In a world of fifty channels (or two hundred channels) you no longer needed to try for a 40 percent market share; capturing 5 or 10 percent of the market could be extremely profitable. And since you no longer had to worry about fairness and equal time, you could cater to a more narrow ideological audience and do very well economically. The formula was simple: inexpensive to produce in studio programs. You could eliminate or minimize the expensive parts of traditional TV news broadcasting—reporters in the field and overseas bureaus—and have a man in the studio with a few guests. To keep people from changing channels, you need to supply lively provocative content: Bill O'Reilly pistol-whipping and cutting the mike of his guests or Glenn Beck spinning his bizarre apocalyptic conspiracy webs.

It is this media landscape that prepared the new post-truth world. The public's inability to make its way through this wilderness of error has led to a virtual collapse of trust in the media, fallen from its height of 72 percent in 1976 to only 32 percent this year. If you don't know what to believe, you will believe anything. And so in this world of extreme distrust and polarization, undocumented stories about Hillary Clinton commissioning murders or being involved in sex-trafficking rings appear to many Americans as credible as well-sourced stories in mainstream media outlets.

This extreme distrust and polarization creates fertile ground for people like Rush Limbaugh to deny the fundamental impossibility of establishing clear facts. "There is no fact-checking," he declared on his show in late September after many in the press published scorecards of the false statements made by Trump during a presidential debate. "The fact that *The New York Times*, and *The Washington Post*, and *USA Today*, and all these other papers and networks now have fact-checkers is for one reason . . . all it is, is a vehicle for them to do opinion journalism under the guise of fairness. Which, if you fall for it, gives it even more power."

Similarly, in Berlusconi's Italy, voters' behavior could be increasingly understood—and perhaps determined by—the media they consumed. The public was almost evenly divided between people who watched Berlusconi's TV stations and those who got their news from other sources. I recall overhearing a conversation among a group of well-dressed young men in a fashionable café in Palermo, Sicily, who were complaining about how unfair it was that Berlusconi had been investigated and indicted on corruption charges multiple times while his chief political opponent, Romano Prodi, had not been indicted once. To them, this was not a sign that there was evidence of widespread corruption and criminal activity in Berlusconi's company and inner circle, but proof that the system was rigged in Prodi's favor.

With the public living in entirely different information worlds, people like Trump and Berlusconi can create their own realities. "I could stand in the middle of Fifth Avenue and shoot somebody and I wouldn't lose voters," Trump said—at a public rally with television cameras rolling. Speaking of his loyal followers, Trump said after winning the Nevada primary: "I love the poorly educated! We're the smartest people, we're the most loyal people."

Donald Trump looks like a total anomaly if you compare him to his immediate predecessors, men like Mitt Romney and John McCain (or even George W. Bush), who were careful never to stray too far from the norms of civil discourse. But if you see him as the heir of Rush Limbaugh and Bill O'Reilly, he falls into a logical progression. For a generation, a large slice of Americans have been fed apocalyptic visions of national decline and heard people like Rush Limbaugh refer to feminists as "feminazis" or deride President Obama as "Barack, the magic Negro." Republican politicians have been happy to stand by and allow right-wing media to push their electorate toward the extremes while continuing to speak the more mild-mannered language of traditional politics. The gap between the real discourse of the right and its official discourse became intolerably great, as was evident during the Republican primaries. Trump leaped in and reduced it to zero and many people, rather than being appalled, were relieved: Here is someone who actually talks the way we do and the way Rush does, rather than like a politician. By comparison, the "respectable" politicians suddenly looked boring and false.

In countries such as the United Kingdom, Germany, and France, large state media companies still dominate the airwaves and act as a kind of referee for civil discourse and establishing commonly accepted facts. It has not prevented extremist movements from developing, but it has meant that the principal conservative parties accept basic realities such as global warming or the fact that the invasion of Iraq was not a rousing success. You cannot simply say anything. Berlusconi and Trump have benefited, in part, from a balkanized media environment where many separate parallel information universes coexist.

To reinforce their alternate reality, both Berlusconi and Trump have made a special target of the so-called mainstream media. (Let's give some credit to Sarah Palin, who anticipated Trump in various ways and has endorsed him for popularizing the term "lamestream" media.) Trump's use of social media to go after his critics is reminiscent of the frequent attacks in the Berlusconi media. One particularly disturbing moment occurred when Trump urged the television operators to point their cameras to a protester at one of his rallies, suddenly making her the object of public rage. It reminded me of a moment when Berlusconi stood side by side with his good friend Vladimir Putin at a press conference in Moscow. When a Russian journalist asked a tough question of Putin (this was several years ago, when such a thing was still possible), Berlusconi made the gesture of firing a machine gun at the woman. In a country where several critical journalists have actually been murdered, this was decidedly unfunny. (Trump and Berlusconi also share a weird kinship with Putin.)

Just recently, Donald Trump indicated that he intended to change the libel laws of this country to keep people from writing bad things about him. "The press is a real problem in this country," he said. "They're worse than the politicians," Trump said, arguing that about 80 percent of the press is corrupt. "They can write anything they want and you cannot sue them, because the libel laws, they essentially don't exist, and one of the things I'm going to do is I'm going to open up the libel laws."

Berlusconi does not have quite the same problem in Italy, where libel laws are far more favorable to plaintiffs. In American libel law, truth is an absolute defense, and in the case of media publishing mistaken information, the plaintiff must show malice or reckless indifference to the truth. In Italy's defamation laws, something can be true and yet defamatory. He and his close associates have sued dozens of journalists and critics over the years, often losing but costing his critics money, keeping them tied up in the courts or reduced to silence.

Life under Berlusconi—as with Trump—has been a kind of race to the bottom. Just when you think he can't go any lower, he surprises you by some new outrageous act, statement, or scandal. One thing I got wrong during the Berlusconi era was believing that the kinds of conflicts of interest represented by Berlusconi would never be tolerated in the United States. Not because of our laws, but because of custom. Given the impotence of our institutions in forcing Trump to divest himself of his business or even to reveal his tax returns, we now realize this is not the case. Berlusconi continually succeeded in lowering the bar for ethical behavior in office and exhausting the Italians' limited capacity for moral outrage. Although it may not make a difference in electoral terms, I think it is extremely important not to accept the new normal as normal.

Life under Trump, as under Berlusconi, is likely to be one of almost constant crisis and unpredictability. The giddiness of public adoration—the narcissistic high of constant media attention—required Berlusconi to create a kind of ongoing reality show whose ratings depended on him continuing to do and say outrageous things. Both Trump and Berlusconi love to pick fights because their popularity depends on the sense of crisis, a world of us-against-them in which the strongman alone can keep at bay the forces of evil. During the Berlusconi (Bush) era, Italian commentators began to use the term "weapons of mass distraction" to describe his style of governance: dominating the news cycle with the latest squabble, bizarre statement, or fake controversy while pulling attention away from the bread-and-butter issues: jobs, health care, education, etc.

Are there lessons from Berlusconi that might help us predict Trump's trajectory and defend against it? Yes and no. Indro Montanelli, a conservative Italian journalist and a fierce Berlusconi critic, said that Italy would need to develop an immunity to Berlusconi by absorbing a certain dose of Berlusconi. Unfortunately, it took seventeen years of constant scandals and economic incompetence for Italians to grow weary of him.

I wish I could say that the Italian public—aided by a valiant and dogged press—woke up and understood how wrong they had been about Berlusconi, how the infinite conflicts of interests he was entangled in paralyzed the country or that his extreme narcissism and short attention span (sound familiar?) made him unusually ill-suited to the task of governance. In the end, I think, it was traditional pocketbook issues that doomed Berlusconi. Like Trump, Berlusconi presented himself as an economic miracle worker. Using his personal wealth as a guarantee, he promised a new era of exceptional national economic revival. Instead, Italy flatlined economically under Berlusconi, ranking year after year among the slowest-growing economies in the world. Although it was not accompanied by much moral outrage, millions of Berlusconi supporters understood that he had failed to keep his promises.

Trump inherits a much stronger economy than Berlusconi did. I suspect that Trump supporters are not likely to be alienated by the self-dealing of a cabinet larded with billionaires or by the tragedy of millions of poor whose lives are likely to get much harder. But if the promise to restore prosperity and jobs to middle America proves to be hollow, I think you can expect a backlash.

THE RIGHT WAY TO RESIST TRUMP

Luigi Zingales

(Italy)

Originally published in *The New York Times* (November 18, 2016)

Five years ago, I warned about the risk of a Donald J. Trump presidency. Most people laughed. They thought it inconceivable.

I was not particularly prescient; I come from Italy, and I had already seen this movie, starring Silvio Berlusconi, who led the Italian government as prime minister for a total of nine years between 1994 and 2011. I knew how it could unfold.

Now that Mr. Trump has been elected president, the Berlusconi parallel could offer an important lesson in how to avoid transforming a razor-thin victory into a two-decade affair. If you think presidential term limits and Mr. Trump's age could save the country from that fate, think again. His tenure could easily turn into a Trump dynasty.

Mr. Berlusconi was able to govern Italy for as long as he did mostly thanks to the incompetence of his opposition. It was so rabidly obsessed with his personality that any substantive political debate disappeared; it focused only on personal attacks, the effect of which was to increase Mr. Berlusconi's popularity. His secret was an ability to set off a Pavlovian reaction among his leftist opponents, which engendered instantaneous sympathy in most moderate voters. Mr. Trump is no different.

We saw this dynamic during the presidential campaign. Hillary Clinton was so focused on explaining how bad Mr. Trump was that she too often didn't promote her own ideas, to make the positive case for voting for her. The news media was so intent on ridiculing Mr. Trump's behavior that it ended up providing him with free advertising.

Unfortunately, the dynamic has not ended with the election. Shortly after Mr. Trump gave his acceptance speech, protests sprang up all over America. What are these people protesting against? Whether we like it or not, Mr. Trump won legitimately. Denying that only feeds the perception that there are "legitimate" candidates and "illegitimate" ones, and a small elite decides which is which. If that's true, elections are just a beauty contest among candidates blessed by the Guardian Council of clerics, just like in Iran.

These protests are also counterproductive. There will be plenty of reasons to complain during the Trump presidency, when really awful decisions are made. Why complain now, when no decision has been made? It delegitimizes the future protests and exposes the bias of the opposition.

Even the petition calling for members of the Electoral College to violate their mandate and not vote for Mr. Trump could play into the president-elect's hands. This idea is misguided. What ground would we then have to stand on when Mr. Trump tricks the system to obtain what he wants?

The Italian experience provides a blueprint for how to defeat Mr. Trump. Only two men in Italy have won an electoral competition against Mr. Berlusconi: Romano Prodi and the current prime minister, Matteo Renzi (albeit only in a 2014 European election). Both of them treated Mr. Berlusconi as an ordinary opponent. They focused on the issues, not on his character. In different ways, both of them are seen as outsiders, not as members of what in Italy is defined as the political caste.

The Democratic Party should learn this lesson. It should not do as the Republicans did after President Obama was elected. Their preconceived opposition to any of his initiatives poisoned the Washington well, fueling the antiestablishment reaction (even if it was a successful electoral strategy for the party). There are plenty of

Trump proposals that Democrats can agree with, like new infra-structure investments. Most Democrats, including politicians like Hillary Clinton and Bernie Sanders and economists like Lawrence Summers and Paul Krugman, have pushed the idea of infrastructure as a way to increase demand and to expand employment among non-college-educated workers. Some details might be different from a Republican plan, but it will add credibility to the Democratic opposition if it tries to find the points in common, not just differences.

And an opposition focused on personality would crown Trump as the people's leader of the fight against the Washington caste. It would also weaken the opposition voice on the issues, where it is important to conduct a battle of principles.

Democrats should also offer Trump help against the Republican establishment, an offer that would reveal whether his populism is empty language or a real position. For example, with Trump's encouragement, the Republican platform called for reinstating the Glass-Steagall Act, which would separate investment and commercial banking. The Democrats should declare their support of this separation, a policy that many Republicans oppose. The last thing they should want is for Mr. Trump to use the Republican establishment as a fig leaf for his own failure, dumping on it the responsibility for blocking the popular reforms that he promised during the campaign and probably never intended to pass. That will only enlarge his image as a hero of the people shackled by the elites.

Finally, the Democratic Party should also find a credible candidate among young leaders, one outside the party's Brahmins. The news that Chelsea Clinton is considering running for office is the worst possible. If the Democratic Party is turning into a monarchy, how can it fight the autocratic tendencies in Mr. Trump?

OPEN SOCIETY NEEDS DEFENDING

George Soros

(European Union)

Originally published in *Project Syndicate* (December 30, 2016)

Well before Donald Trump was elected president of the United States, I sent a holiday greeting to my friends that read: "These times are not business as usual. Wishing you the best in a troubled world." Now I feel the need to share this message with the rest of the world. But before I do, I must tell you who I am and what I stand for.

I am an eighty-six-year-old Hungarian Jew who became a US citizen after the end of World War II. I learned at an early age how important it is what kind of political regime prevails. The formative experience of my life was the occupation of Hungary by Hitler's Germany in 1944. I probably would have perished had my father not understood the gravity of the situation. He arranged false identities for his family and for many other Jews; with his help, most survived.

In 1947, I escaped from Hungary, by then under communist rule, to England. As a student at the London School of Economics, I came under the influence of the philosopher Karl Popper, and I developed my own philosophy, built on the twin pillars of fallibility and reflexivity. I distinguished between two kinds of political regimes: those in which people elected their leaders, who were then supposed to look after the interests of the electorate, and those where the rulers sought to manipulate their subjects to serve the rulers' interests. Under Popper's influence, I called the first kind of society open, the second, closed.

The classification is too simplistic. There are many degrees and variations throughout history, from well-functioning models to failed states, and many different levels of government in any particular situation. Even so, I find the distinction between the two regime types useful. I became an active promoter of the former and opponent of the latter.

I find the current moment in history very painful. Open societies are in crisis, and various forms of closed societies—from fascist dictatorships to mafia states—are on the rise. How could this happen? The only explanation I can find is that elected leaders failed to meet voters' legitimate expectations and aspirations and that this failure led electorates to become disenchanted with the prevailing versions of democracy and capitalism. Quite simply, many people felt that the elites had stolen their democracy.

After the collapse of the Soviet Union, the United States emerged as the sole remaining superpower, equally committed to the principles of democracy and free markets. The major development since then has been the globalization of financial markets, spearheaded by advocates who argued that globalization increases total wealth. After all, if the winners compensated the losers, they would still have something leftover.

The argument was misleading, because it ignored the fact that the winners seldom, if ever, compensate the losers. But the potential winners spent enough money promoting the argument that it prevailed. It was a victory for believers in untrammeled free enterprise, or "market fundamentalists," as I call them. Because financial capital is an indispensable ingredient of economic development, and few countries in the developing world could generate enough capital on their own, globalization spread like wildfire. Financial capital could move around freely and avoid taxation and regulation.

Globalization has had far-reaching economic and political consequences. It has brought about some economic convergence between poor and rich countries, but it has increased inequality within both poor and rich countries. In the developed world, the benefits accrued mainly to large owners of financial capital, who constitute less than 1 percent of the population. The lack of redistributive policies is the main source of the dissatisfaction that democracy's opponents have exploited. But there were other contributing factors as well, particularly in Europe.

I was an avid supporter of the European Union from its inception. I regarded it as the embodiment of the idea of an open society: an association of democratic states willing to sacrifice part of their sovereignty for the common good. It started out as a bold experiment in what Popper called "piecemeal social engineering." The leaders set an attainable objective and a fixed timeline and mobilized the political will needed to meet it, knowing full well that each step would necessitate a further step forward. That is how the European Coal and Steel Community developed into the EU.

But then something went woefully wrong. After the Crash of 2008, a voluntary association of equals was transformed into a relationship between creditors and debtors, where the debtors had difficulties in meeting their obligations and the creditors set the conditions the debtors had to obey. That relationship has been neither voluntary nor equal.

Germany emerged as the hegemonic power in Europe, but it failed to live up to the obligations that successful hegemons must fulfill, namely looking beyond their narrow self-interest to the interests of the people who depend on them. Compare the behavior of the United States after World War II with Germany's behavior after the Crash of 2008: the United States launched the Marshall Plan, which led to the development of the European Union; Germany imposed an austerity program that served its narrow self-interest.

Before its reunification, Germany was the main force driving European integration: It was always willing to contribute a little bit extra to accommodate those putting up resistance. Remember Germany's contribution to meeting Margaret Thatcher's demands regarding the EU budget?

But reuniting Germany on a 1:1 basis turned out to be very expensive. When Lehman Brothers collapsed, Germany did not feel rich enough to take on any additional obligations. When European finance ministers declared that no other systemically important financial institution would be allowed to fail, German chancellor Angela Merkel, correctly reading the wishes of her electorate, declared that each member state should look after its own institutions. That was the start of a process of disintegration.

After the Crash of 2008, the EU and the eurozone became increasingly dysfunctional. Prevailing conditions became far removed from those prescribed by the Maastricht Treaty, but treaty change became progressively more difficult, and eventually impossible, because it couldn't be ratified. The eurozone became the victim of antiquated laws; much-needed reforms could be enacted only by finding loopholes in them. That is how institutions became increasingly complicated, and electorates became alienated.

The rise of anti-EU movements further impeded the functioning of institutions. And these forces of disintegration received a powerful boost in 2016, first from Brexit, then from the election of Trump in the United States, and on December 4 from Italian voters' rejection, by a wide margin, of constitutional reforms.

Democracy is now in crisis. Even the United States, the world's leading democracy, elected a con artist and would-be dictator as its president. Although Trump has toned down his rhetoric since he was elected, he has changed neither his behavior nor his advisers. His cabinet comprises incompetent extremists and retired generals.

What lies ahead?

I am confident that democracy will prove resilient in the United States. Its Constitution and institutions, including the fourth estate, are strong enough to resist the excesses of the executive branch, thus preventing a would-be dictator from becoming an actual one.

But the United States will be preoccupied with internal struggles in the near future, and targeted minorities will suffer. America will be unable to protect and promote democracy in the rest of the world. On the contrary, Trump will have greater affinity with dictators. That will allow some of them to reach an accommodation with the United States, and others to carry on without interference. Trump will prefer making deals to defending principles. Unfortunately, that will be popular with his core constituency.

I am particularly worried about the fate of the EU, which is in danger of coming under the influence of Russian president Vladimir Putin, whose concept of government is irreconcilable with that of open society. Putin is not a passive beneficiary of recent developments; he worked hard to bring them about. He recognized his regime's weakness: It can exploit natural resources but cannot generate economic growth. He felt threatened by "color revolutions" in Georgia, Ukraine, and elsewhere. At first, he tried to control social media. Then, in a brilliant move, he exploited social media companies' business model to spread misinformation and fake news, disorienting electorates and destabilizing democracies. That is how he helped Trump get elected.

The same is likely to happen in the European election season in 2017 in the Netherlands, Germany, and Italy. In France, the two leading contenders are close to Putin and eager to appease him. If either wins, Putin's dominance of Europe will become a fait accompli.

I hope that Europe's leaders and citizens alike will realize that this endangers their way of life and the values on which the EU was founded. The trouble is that the method Putin has used to destabilize democracy cannot be used to restore respect for facts and a balanced view of reality.

With economic growth lagging and the refugee crisis out of control, the EU is on the verge of breakdown and is set to undergo an experience similar to that of the Soviet Union in the early 1990s. Those who believe that the EU needs to be saved in order to be reinvented must do whatever they can to bring about a better outcome.

© Project Syndicate, 2017

Part II

The Middle East

PREPARE FOR REGIME CHANGE, NOT POLICY CHANGE*

N. Turkuler Isiksel

(Turkey)

Originally published in *Dissent Magazine* (November 13, 2016)

It *can* happen here.

Over the past decade, I, along with millions of my compatriots, watched an illiberal populist leader commandeer every lever of power in my country of origin, Turkey, by systematically dismantling constitutional safeguards and intimidating society into submission. Having secured less than half of the popular vote in successive elections, Erdoğan proceeded to jail journalists, activists, judges, prosecutors, generals, and members of parliament. To stay in power, he has reignited a dormant civil conflict, stoked ultranationalist violence, allowed extremist movements to flourish, orchestrated military incursions into two neighboring countries, and shredded the rule of law. In hindsight, the signs of his authoritarian intentions were there all along; many of us just didn't think the republic would succumb so easily.

Those of us who witnessed illiberal populist movements take hold in Turkey, Russia, Hungary, Poland, the Philippines, and elsewhere are watching the election of Donald Trump with a particularly acute sense of foreboding. With this difference: Unlike the

*Originally published as N. Turkuler Isiksel, "Prepare for Regime Change, Not Policy Change," *Dissent Magazine*, Winter 2017, pp. 20–25. Reprinted with permission of the University of Pennsylvania Press.

United States, none of these countries has ever stood out as a beacon of liberty. To many Americans, this means that however autocratic his leanings, Trump's designs will fail. But this is exactly the wrong conclusion to draw. It is precisely such overconfidence in the United States' long and illustrious tradition of liberty that could lull the American public into a false sense of security and facilitate the rapid destruction of that very tradition.

Confidence in the exceptional resilience of American democracy is particularly misplaced in the face of today's illiberal populist movements, whose leaders are constantly learning from each other. Trump has a wide variety of tried and tested techniques on which to draw; already, he has vowed to take pages out of Putin's playbook. Defenders of liberal democracy, too, must learn from each other's victories and defeats. Below are some hard-earned lessons from countries that have been overrun by the contemporary wave of illiberal democracy. They could be essential for preserving the American republic in the dark years to come.

EXPECT THE WORST

Don't look for ways to soothe your sense of alarm, and don't assume that a Trump presidency might turn out less harmful than he has so far indicated. Autocrats almost always turn out worse than they seem before coming to power. A presidential candidate who has uncontrollable fits of rage over perceived slights from a former beauty queen is likely to use every resource available to him to hound his enemies. In the United States, those powers are formidable indeed, ranging from a nuclear arsenal to the boundless surveillance powers of the National Security Agency.

Don't expect the Republican establishment to rein him in, as few Republicans were courageous enough to disavow his candidacy even when he appeared to be losing the election. Now that he controls the most powerful office in the land, expect them to be fully servile.

Don't count on the elaborate system of checks and balances instituted by the founders. James Madison's ingenious machine was designed to withstand the mundane incompetence, greed, and shortsightedness of politicians, but it cannot weather the onslaught of an aspiring tyrant hell-bent on destroying it. Consider that the separation of powers, the primary mechanism Madison envisaged for holding tyranny at bay, is all but irrelevant while Republicans control the House, the Senate, and the presidency—particularly once they get their hands on key federal judicial appointments. All autocrats set about dismantling countervailing power structures, but with the inauspicious ideological alignment of all three branches of government, Trump won't even have to try.

If you trust in freedom of expression to expose the autocratic machinations of a Trump administration, think again. It is no coincidence that Erdoğan and Trump are both litigious in the extreme, regularly using personal lawsuits to bludgeon their critics into quiescence. Autocrats understand that freedom of expression is fragile, and seek to stifle it by hook or by crook. The American free speech tradition is stronger than Russia's or Turkey's, but a hypersensitive, bullying White House press office could easily cow the media into favorable reporting. It does not take much for the deleterious chilling effect of such measures to take hold. Conservative "news" outlets already enjoy overwhelming dominance in the United States, and Trump's singular genius is for manipulating the media. That, after all, is how he fueled the birther movement, which in turn made him into a political force. Finally, he can also be expected, like Berlusconi, to create his own private media empire to shape the "truth" to which a large part of the electorate is exposed.

TIME TO USE THE F-WORD

Progressives err in assuming that the worst danger of a Trump presidency is the reversal of Obama legacy, including the Affordable Care Act, the vindication of the constitutional rights of LGBTQ people, the Iran deal, and progress on climate change. There will surely be an all-out assault on these achievements. But it would a grave mistake to see the obliteration of the progressive policy agenda as the chief danger of a Trump presidency. What we confront is not the usual dogfight between liberals and conservatives. It is a struggle between those who believe in preserving the imperfect but serviceable constitutional system of the republic, and those who will try to undermine it. For all his abhorrent policy positions, a President Cruz could have been counted on to observe the strictures of constitutional democracy, such as the peaceful alternation of power through free and fair elections. Trump gives us every reason to suspect that he will not. If the tactics of Putin, Orbán, Erdoğan, and other populists are any guide, we can expect Trump to do everything he has either threatened to do or baselessly accused the Democrats of doing: fomenting violence and voter intimidation, rigging elections, spying on, prosecuting and imprisoning his opponents, silencing the press, and more.

Like other illiberal populists, Trump is capable of inflicting irreparable damage to this country's institutions within a relatively short space of time. What we therefore have to prepare to resist is not policy change; it is regime change. Above all, we must shake off the "it can't happen here" mentality and seriously contemplate the unprecedented danger Trump represents: that of the United States sliding into a form of fascism. A single cataclysmic event, such as a major terror attack, could hasten this slide. Americans from all across the political spectrum who believe in constitutional democracy must unite to resist it.

PROTEST EARLY AND OFTEN

The experience of Russia and Turkey suggests that the only democratic, nonviolent practice capable of deterring the autocrats is the sight of endless crowds marching: vociferous, tenacious, disciplined citizens claiming ownership over their constitutional liberties and defending the integrity of their political institutions. Erdoğan was never so rattled as he was by the Gezi Park protests that quickly spread all over the country; Putin experienced the only real challenge to his regime during the street demonstrations of 2011 and 2012. In the short term, both movements failed to defang the authoritarian regimes they challenged, not because mass protests were the wrong strategy but because the brutal force commanded by a consolidated authoritarian regime makes it very difficult for such movements to succeed.

This is why it is essential to protest early and often. Citizens of consolidated democracies have absorbed a genteel lesson: If our side loses, we wait our turn until the next election. Under normal circumstances, the internalization of that lesson is essential to democracy's stability. When those in power are poised to destroy constitutional safeguards, however, hanging on in quiet desperation until the next election can be fatal to democracy.

Instead, Americans must tap into their rich and proud tradition of civic resistance, whose highlights are the twentieth-century civil rights movement and protests against the Vietnam War. Civic action needs to begin now. We must claim public squares before Trump takes office, marching in droves and communicating a clear message that his brand of autocracy shall not pass.

Already, citizens are congregating in cities across the countries and a "million-woman march on Washington" is in the works for January 21. Nationwide gatherings take time to organize, but rallies and vigils must become regular events in cities and university campuses across the land. As recent waves of popular mobilization, from Tahrir Square to Gezi Park, have shown, social media enables masses to converge on short notice. Millennials excel at this kind of thing. However, closed-circuit, feel-good moping on social media can never substitute for warm bodies on streets, people who refuse to be dispersed or intimidated. As concerned citizens, we must coordinate with our families, friends, colleagues, students, neighbors, and congregants, making couches available, giving rides, providing child care, covering work shifts, and cooking meals for one another to amplify an effective civic presence. (And let's not forget to continue poking fun at Trump. Autocrats cannot stand humor, which makes it a potent device not just for sapping their egos but also for giving citizens the much-needed solace and encouragement of laughing together.)

FIND STRANGE BEDFELLOWS

Thanks in part to their control over the media, the Russian and Turkish governments persuaded the larger public that the protesters were godless vandals, foreign agents, and marginal types. To combat such a smear campaign, citizens and community leaders must be willing to look past the ideological differences that divide them. These differences have been rendered irrelevant, at least for the moment, by the overriding danger presented by the Trump presidency. This civic resistance must bring together not just progressives of all stripes—including Black Lives Matter activists, unions, and the climate justice movement—but also immigrants, LGBTQ people, conservatives, libertarians, religious groups, veterans, teachers, students, people of all faiths, races, and ethnicities; in short, all those who believe that political disagreements should only be resolved within the framework of constitutional democracy. The good news is that it is easier to unite around opposition to despotism than it is to set out an alternative vision of how government must be run. Still, one of the most potent strategies in the autocrat's toolkit is to sow divisions among the opposition by selectively favoring their causes. Leftists, then, should refuse to be mollified by Trump's anti-free-trade agenda, for instance, or his promise to increase government spending.

BE PEACEFUL AND RESOLUTE

Trump will use the militarized force of US law enforcement against protesters on the ground and will seek to discredit them in the public eye. Already, Milwaukee County sheriff and Trump's potential nominee for Homeland Security secretary David Clarke tweeted that "temper tantrums from . . . radical anarchists must be quelled." (In August, Clarke was quick to call the National Guard into Milwaukee when protests erupted after the police shooting of twenty-three-year-old Sylville Smith.) We must take inspiration from the peaceful momentum built by the Reverend Martin Luther King Jr. and his fellow civil rights activists, and steel our spines against ominous threats that betray the US Constitution's unequivocal guarantees of the freedom of speech, assembly, and association.

Above all, let us not forget that Trump rode to power on the back of public rallies fueled by protest against political power. The tidy, staged meetings in which Hillary supporters wanly pledged to be "with her" failed to match the energy of the Trump movement. The only thing that can arrest the lawless momentum of a Trump regime is the hair of the dog: wave after wave of loud, proud, and peaceful citizens rejecting the hate, vilification, lawlessness, and division for which he stands.

Many Americans have still to discover that nothing boosts civic morale and solidarity like a massive public protest. The act of standing together in a public space and affirming our shared values and our respect for one another is a transformative experience, one that could release the still largely untapped political potential of millennials. In contrast to the Trump rallies in which racist, sexist, and Islamophobic obscenities were chanted by thousands, peaceful mass demonstrations are in order to enact the resilience of American democracy and the inclusive and affirmative ideals for which it stands. The vast majority of Americans who still affirm these ideals need just such an antidote, and they need it now.

TRUMP, SISI, AND A NATIONALIST WORLD

Rana Allam

(Egypt)

January 19, 2017

A version of this piece was previously published in
LobeLog (November 30, 2016)

After a presidential campaign drenched in racism, fear-mongering, division, and ultranationalistic rhetoric, he won. His people woke up the morning after the election divided and driven by anger. Right away, his supporters began to engage in hate speech. Some even took matters into their own hands and physically abused the "other." The state, with its government and people's representatives, was all his. He chose his advisers and ministers from his circle of followers, and there were no voices to hear but his own. His entourage echoed his words, carried out his plans, and applauded his patriotism and courage in crushing the "other." The whole country—Egypt, the United States—descended into despair and division like never before.

This November, democracy advocates in Egypt empathized with their counterparts in the United States after the presidential election. They know a lot about divisive presidents, and they were always the ones to be crushed in the battle for freedom and plurality. Either under Mohamed Morsi (who won on religious grounds) or under Abdel Fattah al-Sisi (who won on a nationalist platform), democratic voices are the ones that pay the price.

Egyptian human rights advocates, who have been fighting repression for years, have long taken issue with the lack of action of a succession of US administrations. But they have also seen the Obama administration suspend military aid to Sisi for two years after his military's power grab. The administration also criticized human rights abuses by the Egyptian regime on several occasions and called for the release of political prisoners. The Obama administration always made a point to appear to defend human rights, although it did not always take action. Still, it was an administration with which democracy and rights advocates could reason.

I remember being part of a peace-builders group of high-profile women from Africa, the Middle East, and Asia as well as two prestigious US organizations. We were to have meetings on Capitol Hill with three Democratic senators and one Republican. The Democrats gave us the time to express our concerns regarding US policy in our respective countries. They took notes and asked questions. The Republican senator sent us one of his junior staff members— maybe an intern—to take a message, although we were scheduled for an appointment. Not that the Democrats had the power to change things, but at least they wanted to know; they listened. The Republicans have a completely different agenda that has nothing to do with human rights or the brutal dictators they support. I was not sure then if such contemptuous behavior was because we were the wrong gender, or the wrong religion, or the wrong skin color. Probably a combination of the three.

President-elect Trump does not care for appearances. Much like Egypt's Sisi, Trump views human rights as an obstacle or, at best, not worthy of attention. It was clear in Trump's praise of brutal dictators and his admiration of their will to kill. To Trump, Iraq's Saddam Hussein was "a really bad guy, but very good at killing terrorists" and Iraq would have been "better off if Hussein remained in power." North Korea's Kim Jong-un and Russia's Vladimir Putin are "strong leaders," and he was indeed "honored" by Putin's praise of him. Sisi, of course, is a "fantastic guy."

But Sisi occupies a special place with the Republicans. In one of the Republican primary debates last year, Sisi was the center of praise by the candidates, who called him "courageous," "tough," and someone who "should be befriended." No wonder that many supporters of Sisi in Egypt were ecstatic when Trump won in November. The media apparatus in Egypt played its role in praising Trump and attacking Hillary Clinton during the election. According to Sisi's cronies in the media, Trump's anti-Muslim stance is directed only at the Muslim Brotherhood, while Hillary was the reason that Morsi came to power.

After Brexit, Theresa May took hold of the United Kingdom. After the November election, white supremacy and Trump took over the United States. The UN Security Council's permanent members are now represented by Trump, Putin, Xi, May, and possibly Le Pen. Who will hold oppressive and brutal regimes accountable? Who will listen to the grievances of human rights advocates?

When the most powerful country in the world falls prey to fear and ultranationalistic sentiment, the whole world will pay the price. When the biggest arms exporter in the world is led by a white supremacist leader, it is indeed catastrophic.

The only way out of the mess is to mobilize civil society. After a short while, the Americans who thought Trump will bring economic prosperity will know the truth—that only the rich will benefit. Similarly, many Sisi supporters now see that all he brought was poverty, and even the rich are suffering from the economic collapse. Protests, as Egyptians can testify, might bring a president down, but that is not a fix for the problem. What brought Trump, Sisi, and their ilk to power are defunct systems that must be changed. The way out of the current crisis rests in the hands of the people.

Unlike Egyptians who have been repressed for decades, the Americans can start their fight from a solid base of rights, freedoms, and democracy. The work of grassroots organizations is crucial in raising awareness, and this should be the main focus for democracy advocates.

The main issue that leads to the rise (and stay) of dictators to power is lack of information, of awareness, of the relevance to daily lives. If it failed at everything else, the Egyptian revolution made that relevance clear. Before the revolution, average Egyptians would blame government employees, maybe even ministers, for their deteriorating living conditions. No one would think of the prime minister or the president; no one made the connection. Some would even think it was God's punishment on them. After the revolution, that connection was made. Now everyone knows who is ultimately responsible for their daily struggles. Awareness is key; it is the start of every meaningful change.

In the years to come it is crucial that Americans become aware of everything their president does and how relevant that is to their lives. It is also crucial to give them the means to voice their grievances. The first thing dictators do is silence the media, then defame civil society organizations rendering dissent voiceless. In his first press conference as president-elect, Trump silenced a CNN reporter, much like Sisi, whose first move was to shut down all opposition newspapers and TV channels. This is the first step to crush dissent. What Americans must do is not let this happen. Dictators, as we have seen for decades in Egypt, take one small step at a time on the road to full oppression. In a country like the United States, these small steps might go unnoticed.

Another crucial step is to unite civil society organizations and movements. It does not help to have a thousand organizations working separately. They must communicate. For example, Egypt has dozens of women's rights groups working on the ground, but they could not mobilize for a big protest or campaign against violence against women or any other issue. Numbers in protests are extremely important; protests or campaigns in many cities at the same time against the same issue are very effective. The need to coordinate and unite when necessary should not be neglected.

One thing also to note is the rise and loudness of extremist voices. Dictators are always extreme, either adopting a religious or nationalistic tone, and this gives a green light to the extremist groups. It would be unwise to laugh them off, or to think that they are not a majority so they are not worth fighting. Extremism spreads like cancer under oppressive, divisive leadership and it must be crushed as it buds. Only the media and civil society can push back, by mobilizing all advocates of rights and freedom, who must use all means to deny extremists even the smallest of gains.

Civil society needs to make a strong presence, on the ground through their grassroots, on the streets, and in the media through statements or protests or even lawsuits against the small actions of the regime to avoid large-scale oppression and divisiveness.

From failures, we learn. It would indeed be wise for Americans to learn from the experiences of those who have lived their entire lives under oppressive, divisive regimes.

WHAT AMERICANS AGAINST TRUMP CAN LEARN FROM THE FAILURES OF THE ISRAELI OPPOSITION

Bernard Avishai

(Israel)

Originally published in the *New Yorker* (November 19, 2016)

For any Israeli who lived through the "mahapach," the electoral "up-ending" of 1977, which brought Menachem Begin's Likud party to power, Donald Trump's victory seems dreadfully familiar. It is not simply that America's most benighted voters—people from the en-titled, stressed majority, people living in what has been euphemisti-cally called the "periphery"—turned a protest vote into an unlikely victory for an extremist leader. It is that this protest seems perma-nent, aimed not at a party or candidate but at the establishment, while the voters themselves seem so fierce in their resentment that they stand to become a permanent fixture of a rightist bloc. During the Obama administration, Likud became an ally of the Republi-cans. Now it seems a model for them.

Many observers believe that Trump's promises will soon prove hollow; that he cannot bring back coal, or tear up NAFTA, or de-port eleven million undocumented immigrants; that he cannot just cut taxes on the rich and produce 4 percent growth. The danger, as liberal Israelis have learned, is that his efforts to fulfill these promises will prove good enough. Likud prime ministers, begin-ning with Begin, have used defense budgets and their command over infrastructure to shore up some of the least employable Israe-lis in brazenly discriminatory ways. The settlements have involved the investment of billions of dollars in low-cost public housing; the roads and bridges connecting them to Israel proper and the West Bank barrier have created thousands of semiskilled jobs. Israeli growth jumped from flat in 1977 to well over 5 percent for three of the next four years. The Israeli left, like American Democrats, has assumed that the poorest voters could be appealed to as a class with social-democratic promises. Likud has proved that what anxious voters from the majority want is paternalistic action, and they don't want the government promising broad measures that seem to advance minorities at their expense.

In the short run, Trump can almost certainly boost defense spending, cut corporate taxes, and invest in significant new infrastructure in Rust Belt states, while cutting Medicaid and other programs more broadly targeted at the poor. His first victory will come when the Republican Congress gives him the hundreds of billions of dollars for roads, bridges, and airports that it did not give President Obama and would never have given Hillary Clinton. These steps, and the subsequent burst of economic growth, will likely prove wildly popular. But this growth, driven by significant added debt, rather than taxation on the rich, will not mitigate inequalities. Eventually it will accelerate inflation, rattle investors, and spike interest rates; by 1984, Israel's rate of growth was less than 1 percent, and inflation was nearly 400 percent.

Nevertheless, the wage earners who were most hurt by Likud's fiscal recklessness stuck with Begin's successor, Yitzhak Shamir, in 1983, and continued to support Likud's hatred of Labor—its banks, its unions, and the allegedly rigged politics that was called "hashita" ("the system"). The jobs, after all, had come with the mockery of elites as unpatriotic; their success was seen as contrived privilege, their skepticism as a lack of religious values, their liberal norms as political correctness. The Trump campaign seems to follow the same pattern on a much larger canvas. Black and Latino minorities are a growing proportion of the American population—about 30 percent. Non-Jews are about 25 percent of Israel, and the Arab population is growing fast. When American voters are polarized along ethnic or tribal lines, and minorities support Democrats "in droves"—as Netanyahu said of Arab-Israeli support for his Labor opponents in 2015—the working-class white majority will continue to turn out against them.

Given Israel's fear of its neighbors, and of Palestinian violence, these polarizing hatreds were easy to exacerbate. Begin's Likud immediately offered circuses along with the bread: a deal with Egypt's Anwar Sadat over the Sinai, followed by a string of "tough" responses to the Palestinians—redoubled settlement activity, and two invasions of Lebanon to root out PLO terror. Who would be surprised if Trump began his diplomatic career by cutting a deal with the Russian president Vladimir Putin over Syria, preserving the Assad regime, and then stepped up the war against ISIS? Who doubts this will enhance his popularity and give him license for permanent military vigilance against "radical Islam"?

When the neediest of the majority make common cause with nationalists, religious zealots, old business opportunists, party hacks, and promoters of armed deterrence, protest votes can morph into political identities. Likud is not purely a party; it is what Trump means by a "movement." The Israeli Labor left could never out-argue the Likud. How does one counter the tautological idea that every new Palestinian attack is the result of Israel not being "strong" enough? Likud's rhetoric—"Islamic extremism," "existential threat"—has become common in the Israeli street. Since the early 1980s, people on the left have admitted having a "rosh katan"—literally, a "small head"—keeping a low profile and focusing on their private lives, because public engagement seemed infuriating and futile.

Few mainstream journalists, consumed as they are with the parties' daily maneuvers, pose much of a challenge to this kind of rhetoric. Israel's private media, aside from *Haaretz*, has become a Likud amplifier; public radio journalists interview one Likud official after another, eager to prove they are close to the action. This tolerance of extremist views, the presumed expressions of a General

Will, is subtle, and almost inevitable. Normalization of this kind can already be felt in Washington. Listen to NPR's David Greene tensely interviewing the Republican blogger Chris Buskirk on Trump's appointment of Reince Priebus and Stephen Bannon to the White House staff. Greene was understandably straining not to be contentious; his guest, newly in demand, left the impression that Trump's appointments were simply the president-elect's version of a team of rivals.

The Democratic Party has some advantages over Israeli Labor in its urgent struggle to win back white working-class voters before their identification with Trumpism hardens. First, there is the party's capacity to renew its leadership, which Labor, working in a system of proportional representation, could not. Last week, Elizabeth Warren gave a characteristically combative speech to the AFL-CIO, saying of Democrats that "as the loyal opposition, we will fight harder, we will fight longer, and we will fight more passionately than ever for the rights of every human being in this country." The Israeli left's sad experience of gradual marginalization suggests that she should not hesitate to make herself the face of the party, raising money, boosting morale, and building a countermovement to the Trump administration.

America also has state governments, which can act alone or in concert to demonstrate the virtues of progressive politics. California, Oregon, and Washington do not need the federal government to build high-speed rail, guarantee abortion rights, or raise the minimum wage. Neither do New York, Massachusetts, Connecticut, Vermont, or Rhode Island. Nor do Illinois or Minnesota, for that matter. These are by far America's richest, most technologically advanced, most culturally urbane states. They are also where economic inequalities are sharpest and social consciousness is highest. Alliances of blue states could act as federated countries, with the wealth and legal latitude to advance in their most important areas.

Still, it is hard for an Israeli liberal to see Trump's victory as a four-year, reversible anomaly. This is the start of a long political struggle. It begins by avoiding consultants and pollsters who think they know what messages will flip counties or appeal to certain demographics, and leaders who believe they can win elections based on their opponents' lack of experience. Is there a big national problem that Democrats can solve, and do they have a leader who embodies the way forward? If we do not answer these questions now, we'll quickly be reduced to reacting to Trump's dramas with small heads.

Part III

Asia

AUTHORITARIAN DEMOCRACY: A PLAYBOOK

Nick Robinson

(India)

Originally published in *Dissent Magazine* (November 14, 2016)

The election of Donald Trump as president of the United States has given a man with clear authoritarian tendencies the keys to the White House. During his presidential campaign Trump repeatedly showcased a strongman leadership style in which he bullied opponents, openly praised autocrats like Vladimir Putin, stoked passions by peddling conspiracy theories, and called on the United States to embrace a nativism that scapegoats minorities, Muslims, immigrants, and outsiders.

But just how great is this danger of authoritarianism? And how would it manifest itself? After all, Americans are proud of their democracy and not likely to quickly give up on elections, courts, or the Bill of Rights. The United States has a vibrant media, civil society, academia, and party system, and there are no plans underfoot to replace the Constitution.

One way to anticipate what Trump's no-holds-barred style may bring to the United States is to look abroad. A number of constitutional democracies from Turkey to the Philippines have recently turned toward leaders with a taste for authoritarianism. In fact, perhaps the clearest parallels of the types of tactics Trump might use come from the world's largest democracy, India, where in the face of violence in Muslim-dominated Kashmir and sharp criticism of his government, Prime Minister Narendra Modi has recently imposed something akin to emergency rule in the country without ever actually declaring an emergency.

Taken together, the set of strategies used by leaders abroad like Modi in India, Erdoğan in Turkey, or Duterte in the Philippines constitute a type of authoritarian playbook. Worryingly, Trump has already threatened to use many of these tactics. What makes these strategies so insidious is that they are generally not unconstitutional or illegal. Instead, these tactics rely on the large amounts of discretion that modern constitutions give to the executive. This discretion is frequently restricted not by laws, but by a set of norms and traditions about what constitutes acceptable executive action. If a leader is willing to undercut these norms, they can effectively shrink the space of dissent. Even though these actions may do immense damage to the social fabric of democracy, since they are legal, there is little courts can do to oppose them.

Five of the most common such tactics include:

1. **Politicizing the prosecution of political opponents.** In countries like India, it is not uncommon for politicians in power, or their allies, to bring cases against opposition politicians. Even if a court ultimately dismisses these charges, these prosecutions drain the resources of one's opponents and cast them under a veil of suspicion. Trump's declared intent to appoint a special prosecutor to pursue a criminal investigation against Hillary Clinton and "lock her up" over her email server fits this pattern. It is not a stretch to imagine that Trump will use politicized investigations or prosecutions against political opponents in the future.

2. **Selective application of the law to the media and civil society.** In India, Narendra Modi's government has audited civil society organizations critical of his government for their taxes or for not complying with regulations around accepting foreign funding. Such actions keep these organizations on the defensive and undermine their legitimacy in the eyes of the broader public. Similar selective application of the law to shut down critics could also be used in the United States. Indeed, after being angered by the *Washington*

Post's coverage of his campaign, Trump threatened he would order the Federal Trade Commission (FTC) to bring an antitrust action against Amazon in retaliation (both the *Post* and Amazon are owned by Jeff Bezos).

3. **The use of libel laws to attack critics.** Even before running for office, Trump was involved in a number of libel actions and he says he will bring litigation against the women who accused him of sexual assault during the campaign. Peter Thiel, who helped fund the lawsuit that ultimately bankrupted Gawker, is one of his primary supporters. Even if Trump ultimately loses the libel cases he brings, the threat of prolonged and expensive litigation can silence both those who wish to speak out about Trump's less savory behavior and the media outlets that dare to report such stories.

4. **Undercutting nonpartisan government institutions.** After a recent coup attempt earlier this year in Turkey, President Erdoğan replaced thousands of civil servants with loyalists. The Turkish example is dramatic, but leaders can also more gradually undermine the nonpartisanship of the state. For instance, in June the Reserve Bank of India's well-respected leader Raghuram Rajan was forced into resigning by the Modi government after he expressed concern over rising intolerance in the country.

In the United States, there are many nonpartisan positions to which Trump might appoint loyalists or from which he may attempt to push out those who do not toe the line—this might be in the Department of Justice, FBI, Federal Reserve, or even the judiciary. Trump has already expressed a desire to "fire" the country's top generals, which he legally could do, thereby turning the military into a partisan entity and reducing its ability to act as a check on Trump's potentially extreme or dangerous orders.

5. **Silence in the face of violence.** Perhaps, however, the most powerful discretionary tool of an authoritarian-inclined leader is not any specific action, but rather his or her silence or inaction in the face of violence or intimidation undertaken in their name. In India, Modi has effectively sat on the sidelines when allies in the media

like Arnab Goswami of *Times Now* (think Sean Hannity on ste-
roids) have branded rights advocates and critical journalists as "anti-
national," or when Muslims have been attacked in the name of the
Hindutva ideology that aided his rise to power.

In the United States, we have already seen minorities, journalists, and university spaces attacked in the name of "Making America
Great Again." The dramatic rise in hate incidents and crimes since
the election has been startling in its breadth. Trump did not order
these attacks, but in refusing to clearly condemn them and continuing to scapegoat minorities, he encourages more such crimes. In a
constitutional democracy extreme elements of the public can frequently do far more to intimidate and wear down critics than the
government itself. Authoritarian-minded leaders know this and use
it to their advantage.

The above is not an exhaustive list of strategies. There are many
others, including tactics that are illegal but difficult to detect—such
as leaking damaging secrets about political opponents (Trump, after all, will now have access to the most sophisticated intelligence
agencies ever created).

Trump is not Modi or Erdoğan or, as some suggest, Hitler—
each of whom themselves sit on a wide spectrum of authoritarianism. Trump's leadership will have its own pathologies that reflect
the man and his context. We should not be surprised, though, to
see him use any of the strategies discussed here, and should anticipate their potentially long-term effects: They may not only allow
him to stay in power for far longer than four years, but could also
do irreparable damage to the country's political fabric and create
an environment in which future American presidents may feel less
constrained to use these tactics themselves.

We now need to find ways to defend our democratic institutions. Concerned citizens should support (financially or otherwise)
civil society organizations and independent journalists, who will
play a critical watchdog role in the Trump era. Meanwhile, lawyers
and judges have a special responsibility to make sure they are not

coopted into providing a veneer of legality and legitimacy to actions that directly undermine our constitutional order.

Significantly, we will also need strong allies within government and the bureaucracy who will put the country and its institutions above their own personal self-interest. For example, when President Richard Nixon ordered his attorney general to fire the special prosecutor who had subpoenaed him to turn over his Oval Office tapes, his attorney general resigned. The attorney general's deputy then also resigned instead of carrying out Nixon's orders. These resignations helped shift public opinion in favor of Nixon's impeachment.

There is a pattern to the strategies authoritarian-leaning leaders use in constitutional democracies. Americans should learn from these tactics and start preparing to respond to them.

SURVIVING TRUMP:
TIPS FROM THE WORLD'S LARGEST
DEMOCRACY TO THE OLDEST

Satyen K. Bordoloi

(India)

Originally posted on SIFY.com, a news website from India
(November 17, 2016)

Dear Citizens of the USA,

While democracy—yours oldest, ours largest—connects us, we have a lot of differences. You may be one-third of our population while we are one-third of your landmass, yet the complexity of language, culture, and viewpoints in India is exponentially greater than in the United States.

Today, however, you are facing what we faced two and a half years back. On November 8, a majority of you, the 47.7 percent who did not vote for Donald Trump (against the 47.4 who did), felt what 68.7 percent of Indians who did not vote for Narendra Modi felt on May 16, 2014, when he became prime minister.

Many Indians felt lost, dazed, and disoriented as they could not fathom that such a divisive figure—much like Trump—with allegations of riots and political assassinations against him, could become prime minister. Many feared the worst but secretly hoped to be proven wrong.

Since that fateful day things have happened in my country, some good and some bad, that had never happened before. The good is something governments are expected to do, but the severity of the impact of the bad brings it to the spotlight.

An open intolerance of the "other" has swept over my great country. On September 28, 2015, in Dadri, Uttar Pradesh, India, a religiously charged mob entered the house of Mohammad Akhlaq, killing him on the mere suspicion of having cow meat. This became one of the first instances of murder and harassment of religious minorities and people of other castes by cow vigilante groups that now have tacit social and even political approval. Many commentators have since sarcastically called out India as the country where a cow is safer than a human.

Good educational institutions have been attacked, students viciously targeted. Conservative ideas and people have been allowed to govern important public offices. A regressive form of patriotism holds court in India; jingoism and warmongering have reached unprecedented levels. A war with Pakistan seems like an inevitability.

On the very day you elected Trump, our prime minister announced a demonetization scheme that instantly made 86 percent of currency notes illegal. Hundreds of millions of people lined up for the next two months outside helpless banks, standing under sun and wind for hours to access their own money. More than one hundred people are reported to have died in the first month alone, standing in these serpentine lines.

Worst of all, millions of people have emerged to blindly defend the prime minister's every transgression and to attack any and every dissenter. Conversation between people with opposite views has almost stopped. It does not help that social media segregates newsfeeds based on what you've liked before, thus widening this gap as we unknowingly begin to live in our own bubbles.

Over the last two and a half years, India has also seen an exponential growth in the battle against those forces spreading hatred and intolerance of minorities, cow vigilante groups, those wanting war with Pakistan, and television anchors like Arnab Goswami, who scream hatred as if their earnings depend on their decibel levels. Pitched against them are activists, students, the disenfranchised, the poor, and the tribal. Millions of minor and major mutinies are being waged every single day. An undeclared civil war is afoot in the country.

These two and a half years have taught us some things, some of which might help you deal with Trump and what he might knowingly, or unknowingly, unleash.

1. **Donald Trump is the symptom**: There's perhaps never been a man with a more reprehensible mind, and with such an absence of grace, to hold such high office in the United States than Donald Trump. Yet he is merely the symptom of a malice, a problem in your society, in your democracy, that you must find and cure. You can remove him, but another like him might take his place. So fight and cure the disease, not the symptom. Introspect, like Michael Moore and Jonathan Pie, and in the future ensure that such things do not come to pass.

2. **He IS your president**: Claiming Trump is "Not My President" will only weaken your democracy. You may not like it, but Donald Trump IS your democratically elected president. He did not stage a coup like the many the United States has sponsored across the world. Stop denying what he is, and keep a close watch to ensure that he delivers not just for those who voted for him, but for the whole nation. Because that is what a democracy is about: a candidate might be elected by one group but after coming to power he or she is supposed to serve everyone. So, hold him accountable, prevent him from implementing anti-people, anti-nation, and anti-world pogroms. Use your democratic powers to hold your president in line. At the same time, if he implements policies that are for the larger common good, go ahead and support him, even if your political leanings are the opposite.

3. **Judge Trump for his actions, not words**: Yes, words are a barometer of a person's soul and, by that definition, Trump might have a very dark soul. But there is a small chance that he might not prove to be as bad as expected. It is hoping against hope, but do trust his reconciliatory victory speech for the time being against your better

judgment. Maybe that was just a sham. Yet he hasn't yet done those things he claims he will. Don't judge him based on future crimes. Right now, give him the benefit of the doubt.

4. **People will show their true colors**: Our prime minister's conservatism and Islamophobia were known to all before he was sworn in to office. This is perhaps what encouraged the people and groups that emerged in my country to unleash chaos in various corners. Murderous cow vigilantes weren't the only ones. People with known bigoted impulses suddenly became heads of institutions and made decisions that fit in the agenda of the ruling party, but against the nation. A large group of people—intellectuals, actors, athletes, directors, etc.—changed colors to suit the ruling dispensation. A lot of problems in my nation have been caused by these people, and not by the prime minister directly. Hence, watch Trump's minions for signs of closet racists and opportunists in all shapes and sizes who will emerge now to lay claim to the pot of gold at the end of the sycophantic rainbow.

5. **Not everyone who voted for Trump is a bigot or a racist**: You may not know it, but your nation is on the brink of a civil war. Even if it isn't literal, divisions in your already fractured society will emerge that could drive people further apart. This has already begun as those who voted for Hillary accuse those who voted for Trump of being bigoted and racist. This is actually a very idiotic simplification of extremely complex human beings and their impulses. We in India have been doing the same thing for two and a half years, and the results have been devastating. Our society has fractured much more because of these blanket accusations. Those who voted for Narendra Modi have gone into their defensive shells after such accusations and became more protective of their leader as their very sense of self became attached to him.

Liberal and left circles are in many ways to blame for this name-calling in India. Do not let that happen in your nation. Remember that not all who voted Trump voted *for* him. Many may only have been voting against Hillary, a candidate who, as Michael Moore articulated, was a warmonger who cozied up to the worst of Wall Street. Don't hate people for voting for Trump. Understand them, engage with them today, understand your own impulses. Don't force fence-sitters to jump on the side of the bigots by you calling them so.

The real battle won't happen out in the open, but rather will be hidden behind other issues. Just to give you one example, our prime minister has constantly tried to take over the independence of the judiciary, especially the Supreme Court. This hasn't raised as big a hue and cry as it perhaps demands, but if he is successful, the stakes for the nation could be devastating.

Hence, while you look at the big picture, do keep an eye on the minor details. If even a portion of your fears come true, you are looking at cataclysms the likes of which your country has not seen in a long time.

If you are on the side of fairness, justice, equality, and liberty—and no matter what your political leanings—a long and bitter struggle awaits you. As the opposite forces are unleashed merely by Trump taking office, your nation will see pitched battles on different fronts.

Keep calm, be patient, preserve your energy, organize, and pick your current battles well. The fight that lies ahead has at stake everything that is beautiful in the world and is a fight for the very soul of your nation.

THE ART OF THE OUTRAGE

Suketu Mehta

(India)

January 17, 2017

Previously published in shorter form as:

Can a Bombay Strongman Explain Trump?
The New York Times (November 10, 2016)

As I watched Donald J. Trump campaigning this year, I thought: I've seen this show before. It was in the 1990s, in Bombay. And the man playing the Trump role was named Bal Keshav Thackeray, the leader of the Hindu nationalist Shiv Sena party, who rode to power on a wave of outrageous stories, bluster, lies, bigotry, and showmanship. He died in 2012, the one man most responsible for ruining the city I grew up in. The road to understanding Trump, and what might become of America, might just lie through understanding the rise of Thackeray and what became of Bombay.

Trump has been compared to other strongmen, like Putin, Berlusconi, or Duterte—charter members of the International League of Strongmen that's menacing the planet these days. But in Bombay, we've been familiar with the type since the 1960s, which is when Thackeray first formed his political party, the Shiv Sena.

Thackeray began his career as a political cartoonist; he had a gift for outrageous parody. His own appearance was a caricature of a Bollywood guru; in his later years he took to wearing dark shades, an orange robe, and a necklace of holy beads, holding a Cohiba in one hand and a glass of warm beer in the other. He liked to refer to himself as "the Supremo."

Thackeray was a master of the art of outrage, of politics as performance. He would castigate his opponents as "vampires," "a sack of flour," and various untranslatable epithets like calling South Indians "yandu gundus." Periodically he would express admiration for Hitler, immediately attracting thousands of news pages of free publicity. He regularly called for books and films that he felt were antithetical to Hindu values to be banned. Enraged by his invective, his legions would go out and beat up artists and journalists.

Though there are important differences between the two—Thackeray was not a businessman, born with a silver foot in his mouth, like Trump—their base was remarkably similar in its political contours. The people he represented were the native Maharashtrians, the "sons of the soil." His enemies list varied from year to year, from communists, to South Indians, to Gujaratis, to Muslims, and, most recently, to North Indians. Working-class Maharashtrians felt excluded from the boomtown that Bombay was becoming, as it turned from a manufacturing to a financial and services-based economy. They were under threat both from the cosmopolitan elites who had the real money, as well as from the North Indian migrants who competed with them for low-skill jobs.

Thackeray promised to restore their jobs, by threatening mob violence against industrialists who hired anyone else. He promised to make Maharashtra great again by reversing the clock: his idol was the sixteenth-century warrior-king Shivaji, who held the Muslim empires at bay. He demanded the requirement of a visa to enter Bombay. He played fast and loose with the facts, claiming that the constitution allowed imposition of a ban on outsiders. His party newspaper, *Saamna,* was the Breitbart of its time, chock full of fake news about Muslims, outsiders, celebrities—anyone the Supremo took a dislike to.

Bombay had always been a tolerant, cosmopolitan city; the riots of Partition in 1947 devastated Delhi and Calcutta but barely touched Bombay, which took in massive waves of refugees and accommodated every faith. But in 1992, after the destruction of the Babri Masjid in North India by a Hindu mob, Bombay erupted in mass riots in which nine hundred people, most of them Muslims, lost their lives. Thackeray, according to a judicial inquiry, led his troops "like a veteran general" in organizing the attacks. Like Trump, Thackeray had scant respect for the judiciary. "I piss on the court's judgements," he declared. "Most judges are like plague-ridden rats against whom direct action must be taken." The riots solidified the Hindu vote behind Thackeray and propelled his party into power, in the city and the state.

After Thackeray's riots, Muslims were pushed to or sought out their own ghettoes. In retaliation for the riots, the dons of the Muslim underworld planted ten bombs that together killed 317 people, Hindu and Muslim alike. The tensions continue to this day, stoked by the Shiv Sena's more respectable coalition partner, Modi's Bharatiya Janata Party.

As soon as the Sena assumed office, at the state and city level, it got into bed with the very elites it had scorned, dispensing special favors for well-connected industrialists. Thackeray loved big business, and big business loved him; the Sena-controlled trade unions were much more malleable than the left-controlled ones.

When I went back to Bombay in 2008, I found the Shiv Sena street fighters I had known in the 1990s, along with the Muslim gangsters they had battled, all working in real estate. They had been hired by developers to extort slum dwellers into consent to their houses being razed, in exchange for shabby tower blocks under a government program. The alligators in the Bombay swamp had never feasted better.

Thackeray never held a political office, not even in his own party. It was essential for Thackeray's appeal that he was bigger than politics. "I hate politics," he said, and bragged that he controlled his ministers by "remote control."

I went to interview Thackeray in his bungalow, which had a

perennial line of favor-seekers waiting in the antechamber. They could be Bollywood stars, the president of Enron, gangsters, or clerks. At one point during the interview, he launched, unprompted, into an extended soliloquy about rats in Bombay. His answers had no relationship to my questions; they were simply stray thoughts that seemed to occur at that particular moment. It was a mismatch of scale: this small-minded man controlling this enormous city.

Thackeray had no use for theories or data; he was all about action, or the illusion of action. "I like people who can get things done!" a sign in his office proclaimed. His solutions to the city's vast problem were precise and petty: rename Bombay to Mumbai, ban Valentine's Day, increase water flow in the city's hydrants to better enable the flushing out of rats.

But he was the most powerful man in the city. Because, like Trump, he knew how to tell a good story.

The 2016 election was about the triumph of stories over numbers. Hillary had the most sophisticated algorithms spitting out numbers in her Brooklyn command center; Trump went with his gut. He got up on the stage and, like Thackeray, told stories, ripping yarns. The audience laughed, they cried, and then they voted.

I teach journalism at New York University, and the election was an epic fail for my profession. Neither I nor a single one of the respected journalists I know predicted the result—as, in the 1980s, nobody in elite Bombay could predict that Thackeray's party would ever win power. Throughout Trump's candidacy, we were outraged but also entertained by his tweets. I would look at my phone first thing in the morning, wondering, "What crazy thing came out of Donald's head at 5 a.m.?"

In the months leading up to the election, so many of us sought comfort in the data; we looked at our Fivethirtyeight.com or Upshot several times a day, and were reassured when as late as the morning of the election, were assured that Hilary had an 85 percent chance of winning.

But human beings are too sophisticated, too nuanced, too

complex, to be captured in numbers. We respond with our head to numbers; we respond with our heart to stories. God speaks to us in stories. The scriptures of every faith are collections of stories, not assemblages of data: "In a recent poll conducted by St. Peter, 64.5% of people surveyed believed that they should behave with others as they might wish others to behave towards them; 13% disagreed; and 22% had no opinion."

Trump understands and Thackeray understood the power of stories, and spoke not in policy, but in parables. "I met a fella who told me a story . . ." A populist is, above all, a gifted storyteller. That doesn't mean that the story he's telling is true. It just means that it is entertaining: a false story, well told. At this point in our great democracy, most voters are bored, and they don't respond well to policy statements. Half of all eligible American voters didn't even show up at the polling booth.

I remember attending a Hillary rally in Philadelphia, tacked on to the end of a Katy Perry concert, like the obligatory government documentaries about dams and wheat production attached to Bollywood screenings in the theaters of my youth. I can't remember a single word of what the candidate said, so anodyne was the content, so poll- and focus-group tested were the lines.

The responses of both candidates to an invitation from a Bollywood awards function in New Jersey demonstrated their vast differences in message delivery. Hillary: "In the melting pot of New York and across America . . . tonight's event further expands our social, cultural, and artistic boundaries . . . honor and strengthen the enduring links between South Asia and America. . . ." Trump: "It's a weakness. . . . I love the beautiful Indian actresses. There's nothing like them."

Every year during the Hindu festival of Dussehra, Thackeray would get on the stage at Shivaji Park and deliver a performance lasting several hours, part stand-up comedy, part paranoid conspiracy theory, part scurrilous mockery of his political opponents. Hundreds of thousands of his followers waited for hours to hear him speak, and when he did, they cheered, laughed, engaged in frenzied call-and-response. He never even used a written text, let alone a tele-prompter. A high, or low, point was his mockery of Sonia Gandhi, the Congress party leader. Thackeray would pull a saree over his head and mimic the Italian in a high falsetto, mocking her fum-bling Hindi. Just as, a few decades later, Trump mocked his female opponent.

At the rallies, each attendee felt like Thackeray was speaking to him personally. A Shiv Sena activist told me that, after the riots, Thackeray had "powertoni": a contraction of "power of attorney," the awesome ability to act on someone else's behalf, to sign docu-ments, or to have people killed. The Trump supporters now feel like the Sena supporters: Through him, the formerly powerless fac-tory workers in Ohio and coal miners in Kentucky have powertoni. Every time your hero, your attorney, humiliates the good and the great, you feel a swell of pride, you feel, in your shabby house with the leaky roof, that you've got a measure of power, in Manhattan, in Washington.

Another Shiv Sena activist talked to me with great pride about the time every year on the Supremo's birthday when they went to his bungalow. "We watched all the big people, ministers, business people, bow and touch his feet." His friend added, "Michael Jackson only meets presidents of countries, he came to meet [Thackeray]." Indeed, in 1996, Jackson stopped over in his house on the way to the airport and used the toilet; Thackeray proudly led reporters after-ward to the sanctified bowl.

Just as now, we watch a long line of America's richest or most fa-mous people line up in Trump Tower to kowtow before the man they were ridiculing weeks ago. When the Bollywood superstar Sanjay Dutt, son of the principled member of Parliament Sunil Dutt, who resigned in disgust after the riots, was jailed for his involvement in the bombings, the only man who could get him bail was Thackeray. When Dutt was released from jail, his first stop, even before he went home, was to go to the bungalow with his father and touch the

Supremo's feet. Thackeray gloated over the pictures' release, just as Trump can be seen gloating in the pictures of a groveling Mitt Romney at Jean-Georges, begging for forgiveness and a job.

Bombay's attention, ever since the riots, has been focused on security, on law and order—on bombs and gang wars, on the always looming threat of political mob violence. This means that other areas of governance have suffered enormously. The city is a disaster: the traffic unendurable, the air unbreathable, the housing unaffordable. But the politics of performance continues: Recently, Prime Minister Modi, instead of tackling the awesome urban problems of the city, laid the foundation stone for a 630-foot-tall statue of Shivaji in the sea off Bombay. At a time when the city desperately needs money for clean air and functioning trains, all the politicians have come together to approve spending half a billion dollars on the outsize boondoggle.

Thackeray created a climate of fear in Bombay; there were truths that could only be told in whispers. He claimed to be a guardian of Hindu morals, calling for a ban on Valentine's Day, but there were stories about his personal life that every rickshawallah knew, yet no paper dared to print. When I verified the substance behind some of these stories and tried to put them in my book, my Indian publisher responded: "We can't print that."

"Why not?" I responded. "I'm not afraid of getting sued."

"It's not that they'll sue us. They will burn down my warehouse."

The Muslims who were attacked in the riots were from all social classes and have never recovered from that betrayal: They had been made to feel like foreigners in the city in which they were born and raised. Their killers are still walking free; I interviewed several of them, who bragged about the killings, knowing that they were untouchable because they had "powertoni."

I don't know if Trump's election will lead to rioting and mass violence. But, like Thackeray, his ability to sell a bad story well, and our voracious need to be entertained, have already ensured that the well has been poisoned, and the walls are already coming up—not on our southern border, but between city and village, red and blue state, white and nonwhite, male and female, native and immigrant. Bombayites never imagined that Thackeray's riveting speeches could lead to dead bodies on the streets. Since the election, hate crimes have risen by 115 percent in New York, Trump's birthplace and my home since I was fourteen. What happens if the violent incitement of Trump's campaign continues into his presidency?

So what can those of us who are outraged about Trump do? We need to reclaim control of the story, to look past the numbers and rescue the true story from the false story. But for that we need candidates who can tell the truth with equal passion, directness, and narrative appeal: "The entire planet is in peril. Our lives, and our children's lives, are at stake."

But it doesn't just have to be a negative message. The success story of New York, home to all the peoples of the world, is something that should be celebrated and emulated all across the country. We need to give Americans a sense of confidence in the world, not a fear of it; a sense of pride in what the country has become under Obama—a chance of greatness for all Americans, not just the white ones.

The story we're selling has to be honest. And part of that honesty is telling coal miners and factory workers, "Your jobs are never coming back, at least not in the form your parents had them. But what the country can and should do is train you to do the kind of jobs that the twenty-first century needs." We have to tell them: "It's not Mexicans and Muslims that stole your future. It's Manhattan, in the offices of the bankers who serve no public good besides moving piles of money around. And guess who they're backing, by fair means or foul: your false prophet, Trump."

As journalists, we have to do our dharma. Somewhere out there, somebody has a copy of Trump's tax returns. Somewhere out there, somebody has documentation about Trump's dealings with the Russians. Somewhere out there, there's a Trump sex tape, because a narcissist like Trump doesn't have sex without, at some point, wanting to look at himself having sex.

But even more important, we have to expand the circle of people who our journalism reaches. We need to get up from our desks and go out in the country, not put out three blog posts a day aggregating content that others have produced. My friends and I in New York need to spend less time trying to get published in the *New York Times* and *New Yorker* and more in the *Green Bay Press-Gazette* and the *Scranton Times-Tribune*. Let's take the story to them. Let's tell it like it is: Powertoni to the People.

A WARNING FOR AMERICANS FROM A MEMBER OF PUSSY RIOT

Jim Rutenberg

(Russia)

Originally published in *The New York Times* (December 4, 2016)

MIAMI BEACH—On Tuesday, Donald J. Trump wrote on Twitter that people who burn the flag should be punished with "perhaps loss of citizenship or year in jail!"

Two days later, I went to a little cafe here to meet with Nadya Tolokonnikova of the Russian punk band and activist art collective Pussy Riot. The group's 2012 guerrilla performance at the Cathedral of Christ the Savior in Moscow, which viciously mocked Vladimir Putin and the Russian Orthodox Church, resulted in a two-year prison sentence for Tolokonnikova and another of its members.

I had been in South Florida for family reasons and when I saw that Tolokonnikova was swinging through Miami for Art Basel, I immediately reached out to her. I'd come to view her as an emissary from a dystopian political-media environment that seemed to be heading our way, with governmental threats against dissent, disinformation from the presidential level, and increasingly assertive propagandists who stoke the perception that there can be no honest arbiter of truth.

It's what Tolokonnikova was protesting, and it's what led to her brutal internment, which lasted more than twenty months and ended in 2013.

Leading up to Tolokonnikova's trial, Russian news reports carried suggestions that she and her bandmates were pawns of Hillary

Clinton's State Department or witches working with a global satanic conspiracy—perhaps linked to the one that was behind the September 11, 2001, attacks, as lawyers for one of their offended accusers put it. This is what we now call "fake news."

Pussy Riot became an international symbol of Putin's crackdown on free speech; of how his regime uses falsehood and deflection to sow confusion and undermine critics.

Now that the political-media environment that we smugly thought to be "over there" seems to be arriving over here, Tolokonnikova has a message: "It's important not to say to yourself, 'Oh, it's okay,'" she told me. "It's important to remember that, for example, in Russia, for the first year of when Vladimir Putin came to power, everybody was thinking that it will be okay."

She pointed to Russian oligarchs who helped engineer Putin's rise to power at the end of 1999 but didn't appreciate the threat he posed to them until they found themselves under arrest, forced into exile or forced into giving up their businesses—especially if those businesses included independent media critical of Putin (see Berezovsky, Boris; Gusinsky, Vladimir).

Of course, the United States has checks, balances, and traditions that presumably preclude anything like that from happening, she acknowledged as we sat comfortably in sunny Miami Beach while it played host to a celebration of free expression (Art Basel).

"It is a common phrase right now that 'America has institutions,'" Tolokonnikova said. "It does. But a president has power to change institutions and a president moreover has power to change public perception of what is normal, which could lead to changing institutions."

As if to make her point, later that day the informal Trump adviser Corey Lewandowski declared that the *New York Times'* executive editor, Dean Baquet, "should be in jail." In October, the *Times* published an article about leaked pages from Trump's 1995 state tax returns.

If influential advisers to Mr. Trump continue to so loosely issue jail threats to journalists for doing their constitutionally protected work after Inauguration Day, well, that's a big change to the institution of the presidency in my book, as well as in the one the founders wrote.

None of it is all that shocking to Tolokonnikova, who at twenty-seven has seen this music video before.

When I met her, she was relaxed, wearing a white T-shirt emblazoned with the words "Wild Feminist."

She was planning a lecture that night urging artists to become more engaged and pick up where the politically conscious punk bands like the Dead Kennedys left off—their messages largely lost in the music of corporate-label imitators who hardly said boo through the debates over two wars, the Great Recession, and racially charged police shootings.

So it was that some of the most provocative musical statements of the presidential election came from the Russian women of Pussy Riot, whose work is about things much bigger than their own careers.

They have been working on their English-language music with Dave Sitek of TV on the Radio and the producer Ricky Reed, Tolokonnikova said.

The last video they released, in late October, was called "Make America Great Again." It showed fictional Trump agents in red armbands raping and torturing in a campaign against Muslims, Mexicans, women who have abortions, gays, and lesbians.

It was certain to offend. But it wasn't illegal, at least not here—at least not yet.

And it was a modest Russia-in-America answer to the more voluminous pro-Trump propaganda Putin exported to the United States. Some arrived through his sophisticated state-financed news networks (one, Sputnik, featured #CrookedHillary hashtags on its Twitter feed). And if assessments by the United States intelligence community are correct, some came through state-supported Internet skulduggery.

Tolokonnikova said she became more involved here because the stakes were bigger than one country.

"What happens in one country has a huge influence on what's going on in other countries," she said. "So, I didn't want Donald Trump to be elected because it would obviously encourage authoritarian politicians around the world to be more authoritarian, and it did." (To wit, President Rodrigo Duterte of the Philippines claiming without substantiation that Trump had endorsed his murderous drug crackdown.)

Yet as the Web enables Putin to spread propaganda that encourages nationalist movements to campaign for walls and isolation—most recently, it is claimed, in Italy, where a referendum was held on Sunday—it also breaks down the cultural barriers between countries.

There are places in Russia where the Internet provides a rare route to real news, given that Putin has effectively pressured so much of Russia's independent journalism out of existence on television, on radio, and in print.

But truth cannot break through if people never find it or believe it when they do. And the problem in Russia is the same one we're seeing here, Tolokonnikova told me. "A lot of people are living really unwealthy lives so they have to work not one but two jobs, so they don't have time to analyze and check facts, and you cannot blame them," she said.

And, after so many years in which the "lift-all-boats" promises of globalization didn't come to pass, she said, "they don't trust bureaucrats, they don't trust politicians, and they don't really trust media."

That's why the top Russian propagandist Dmitry K. Kiselyov can assert that "objectivity is a myth" and, here in the United States, the paid CNN Trump-supporting contributor Scottie Nell Hughes can declare: "There's no such thing, unfortunately, anymore, of facts."

When there is no truth, invasions are "liberations" and internment camps are "relocation centers."

But, as Tolokonnikova said, "There is always a way if you really want to tell the truth."

Doing so, for her, has come at a cost, even after prison. Informal Cossack security forces beat her and other Pussy Riot members as they prepared to perform in Sochi during the 2014 Olympics. That same year, a youth gang attacked her with trash and a green antiseptic chemical in Nizhny Novgorod, where she was protesting prison conditions. The men were clearly identifiable but, she said, police made no arrests.

Tolokonnikova has also cofounded a news site called Media Zona. She said it avoids opinion so that readers would accept it as a just-the-facts counter to disinformation.

"You are always in danger of being shut down," she said. "But it's not the end of the story because we are prepared to fight."

Her counsel for United States journalists: You'd better be, too.

IN CASE OF POLITICAL CATASTROPHE

Nadya Tolokonnikova of Pussy Riot

(Russia)

On January 20, 2017, the day of Donald Trump's inauguration as President, Nadya published an op-ed for Billboard.com, summarizing her tips for survival under a Trump regime.

* * *

In case of political catastrophe.

1. **Don't panic.**

2. **Stay focused.** Though don't focus just on yourself. The question "How would I survive under a Trump presidency" is false at its core: Think about those who are the most vulnerable, who are going to suffer from a Trump presidency the most. Find ways to help them. And then—oh, miracle!—you'll notice that your own political anxiety is fading away.

3. **Learn your history.** Figure out what you can do; follow your plan and your social justice dream—day by day, step by step.

4. **A is for Activist: a social justice's hustler.** Think beyond egocentrism—stop asking yourself how you're going to change the world. Hey, you cannot change the world alone. But go hustle for justice anyway; make your input, your energy, an idea, an impulse. It will make a difference.

5. **Be thankful for any achievement.** Even if it seems small to you. Look around: You could either hate all those people and turn your

life into a hell, or you could love them, and it'll bring heaven to the earth.

6. **If your government is a pile of trash, build your own guerrilla government.** Build and participate and support the network of alternative institutions, organizations, initiatives. We'd better be smart and fast in creating effective alternatives in those areas where government and corporation fails: health care, education, media.

7. **Fight for your right.** Obstacles should not discourage you from action. The opposite is truth: Let obstacles motivate you.

8. **Respect your mistakes.** Even a total disaster could teach you some important lessons. Like: You got Trump and it royally sucks, but it may be a sign that it's time for a radical political analysis—it's time to analyze systemic political diseases. It's time to think about 1 percent and 99 percent dialectics. It's time to question—how it's possible that many human beings are treated in our society as disposables, based on class, race, sex, religion. Think about mass incarceration. Imagine for a second what it means to be released from prison and be rejected everywhere, to feel like a second-class human being.

9. **Don't sit around like the world owes you something.** Give yourself to the world, be a human gift to the world—cherish it, love it, share yourself with it. And be attentive and thankful enough to notice gifts and miracles that the world sends you back.

10. **I want to exist, therefore I protest.** Proclaim—loudly—your presence. Our scream is loud. Sometimes it suffocates us because we run out of breath. We break our voices when we're trying too hard. But it's our price to pay. When you want to put something on fire, you need to burn yourself. A miracle that happens just when you wish for it is so real so you could eat it for breakfast instead of eggs.

WHAT THE TRUMP ERA WILL FEEL LIKE: CLUES FROM POPULIST REGIMES AROUND THE WORLD

Melik Kaylan

(Various populist regimes)

Originally published in *Forbes* (January 10, 2017)

This column is about what life will be like under Trump, based on discernible patterns in other countries where populists gained power, especially those with possible murky Russian ties. I write this not as the kind of airy opiner now ubiquitous via the Internet—just one more shrill partisan voice in the noise—but as a professional with specific two-decades-long experience in the subject. Experience on the ground that is, as a reporter and commentator. I have now covered upwards of a dozen countries that have buckled under the emergent wave of populist leaders, from the Far East to the Mideast to Europe and the Americas. Many of the countries have done so quite democratically at first. That emergent wave has crashed onto US shores in a fashion thoroughly precedented abroad.

Recently, I wrote about how I'd seen all the tricks in the Trump campaign before, actually in Tbilisi, Georgia, during the 2012 national elections when the pro–United States candidate lost to a pro-Russian populist. At that time, no one was ready to believe the Russians capable of influencing Western-style elections. Many still don't, even after Trump. We now have enough experience with populists in power in the West and elsewhere to guess intelligently at what's to come in the United States; what life will feel like under Trump.

Here is a checklist to compare against in the coming months and years. We will all be happier if none of this comes to pass but the weight of evidence suggests the worst. Equally, none of this implies that supporters of Trump don't have legitimate issues on their side that, sadly, other politicians won't address—which, not incidentally, is how populists come to power.

CONSTITUTIONAL CHAOS

Already the intelligence services and Trump have squared off. Think about that for a long moment. Then think about what Trump will do. He will appoint new chiefs. They will fight with their rank and file. He will try to downsize and defund. There will be pushback. Imagine what that will look like in the media.

Then there's the Constitution's Emoluments Clause, which, according to various experts, requires Trump to resign from his businesses. He won't fully. His kids certainly won't. His kids will also occupy indefinable White House positions with disproportionate power, raising all manner of nepotism questions.

For a long while, Trump will ignore his more-or-less respectable cabinet chiefs and get things done via nonaccredited unofficial advisers. Picking through the legal minefield, the courts—and ultimately the Supreme Court—will be very busy. So, think about vacancies on the Supreme Court.

Watch Republicans in Congress divide endlessly over the issues. There will be incessant all-against-all confusion in America's institutions—as there was in the very process of the election. As Miklos Haraszti warns in his cri de coeur in this volume, we cannot put faith in the rectifying force of democratic institutions. No "normalization" happens under the corrective effect of institutions. Rather, institutions themselves get eroded.

All this chaos—*cui bono*? Confusion and uncertainty creates a yearning for strongman rule.

EVERYTHING IS EQUAL AND OPPOSITE

At first it was Trump forecasting doubts on electoral fairness. After the election, it was Hillary's turn. First the FBI seemed to take Trump's side. Then the CIA took the opposite side. Right-wingers went with Putin over their own national security agencies. Progressive types unprecedentedly sided with national security. Suddenly up is down, down is up. Everything can become its reverse; moral equivalency will reign.

Trump's conflicts of interest? Answer: What about the Clinton Foundation? Trump's (and Kissinger's) connections to Russia? Answer: What about the Clinton Foundation? Kremlinologists of recent years call this "whataboutism" because the Kremlin's various mouthpieces deployed the technique so exhaustively against the United States. So, Putin commits Georgia, Crimea, Donbass, MH17, Olympic doping, poisoning and killing of opponents, Assad, Aleppo, etc.? Answer: What about Iraq and Libya?

The suspicious similarity between Kremlin propaganda and Trump propaganda cannot possibly mean that the Kremlin influences the Trump campaign? Surely not. Preposterous notion. But just in case the patterns don't go away, remember: The Kremlin's goal is not merely to create national bifurcation. The goal is to create confusion of allegiance, of trust, of truth, loss of faith in the open society, in the very epistemology of empirical fact. You'd think such a quasi-metaphysical inversion of all certainty couldn't be deliberately achieved. You'd have to be paranoid to believe that.

Believe it, because we have the established record in other countries, in Russia, in Georgia, in Turkey, in Poland, and in Hungary. As Harastzi relates from the Hungarian experience: "Populists govern by swapping issues, as opposed to resolving them. Purposeful randomness, constant ambush, relentless slaloming and red herrings dropped all around are the new normal. Their favorite means of communication is provoking conflict. They do not mind being hated. Their two basic postures of 'defending' and 'triumphing' are impossible to perform without picking enemies." Similarly, in Turkey, every day furnishes recurrent narratives of conflict, arrests, and firings, whereby the entire country lives in constant turmoil and confusion. Meanwhile Erdoğan consolidates power.

CURBING THE MEDIA

Already, the US news media serves separated groups of true believers while citizens in the thinning center drift to either side. Few CNN watchers follow Breitbart and vice versa. In short, the country cannot agree on what actually happened at any given time. The fight is over reality itself. If people treat every fact as partisan, facts cease to be facts. In the confusion, the populist leader attacks opposition media for causing the confusion. Chávez and Maduro blamed "saboteurs" for shortfalls in foodstuffs at supermarkets. In a more extreme case the ruling party in Turkey provoked terror and then used each incident to curb press freedom as a way of curbing terror. From Cairo to Moscow we've seen this same scenario: Government quickly accuses the press of abetting terrorists by revealing too much. Let us hope that Trump's tenure doesn't coincide with a sustained wave of terrorist acts. Let us hope that the Kremlin keeps this method of interference and provocation undeployed.

You might argue that the US Constitution explicitly protects independent news media. The United States is not Turkey or Russia. You can't fine or close down top newspapers or their reporters. No, but you can jail journalists for holding out on information crucial to national security. Already, we see the Trump administration asking NBC to reveal its sources of high-level leaks from the intelligence community. Such legal disputes over media freedoms can rumble on endlessly, causing clouds of distraction. But the real war between Trump and the media will unfold elsewhere, along other stealthier vectors. Assume that Moscow has our digital communication records—and I mean most of us—going back many years: emails, health details, banking details, even telephone calls. Now you know why those mysterious hacks of large data banks happened repeatedly, for so long.

Expect specific anti-Trump or anti-Putin figures to find themselves swathed in personal scandals, from journalists to politicians to entertainers. See what was done to such staunch anti-Kremlin investigative journalists such as Anne Applebaum (a contributor to this volume) and the Finnish journalist who probed Russian trolls, Jessikka Aro. In Poland, it took the form of audiotapes of politicians chatting unguardedly at a restaurant they favored, taped throughout many months and then released on the Web. All resigned. The government fell. Populist government took over. In Turkey, it was emails and cell phone chats by any and all possible independent thinkers to consolidate power before elections.

NEW DISTRACTIONS

The news media's compulsion to swarm all over certain news events—shootings, bombs, personal scandals, leaks—poses a genuine risk to the media itself. Its clout weakened by fragmented niche audiences, the media only unites in covering such topics en masse, which then offers opportunities for genuinely effective and damaging manipulation from abroad, some of it highly convoluted. Watch out for ultra-salacious leaks about Donald Trump or his personal entourage that prove partly or wholly false. Such fake news will precede or render ineffectual real revelations.

In addition, you find in populist regimes worldwide the discovery of hitherto untapped areas of news. Duterte of the Philippines hit on the drug problem. Trump has suddenly unearthed an entirely fresh news source in car companies' plans to invest abroad. Trump invented the Mexico wall issue, which will turn into a Klaxon-loud distraction resource for him at every opportunity. In Georgia, Russia, Turkey, and elsewhere people woke up one day to find that, apparently, their national religion needed defending from inscrutable forces, according to their demagogue leaders. In Thailand, the regime's sentimental oratory wraps itself in the perpetually threatened flag of King and (Buddhist) Temple. Also in Thailand, the premier of the army-led regime has sung and released a mawkish patriotic pop song urging unity and positive support—to massive media coverage ad nauseam. He has auto-created his own news cycle, conflated entertainment and politics, an accusation oft leveled at Trump. We all see that Donald Trump's tweets also serve as news distraction, his form of proactive self-leaking.

In a memorable recent interview on MSNBC, media guru Michael Hirschorn, formerly the programming director who brought reality shows to VH1, talks of Trump's reality TV approach to politics. Money quote: "in reality TV you don't resolve disputes; you foster them endlessly to retain public attention."*

UNNERVING FANTASYLAND

Sometimes populists do invoke issues that have become urgent, issues that genuinely exercise citizens but that conventional politicians or media simply haven't dared to address. Keep in mind, though, Miklos Haraszti's warning in this volume: There is no plan to resolve such issues, merely to keep them active and inflammatory. The aim is to keep it all on the boil, crisis merging into crisis, with the strong leader dominating and stoking the noise. There will be something fresh every day, from Monica Crowley's plagiarism to the fashion choices of the first lady. Behind the noise, there will be only more noise. Some demagogic quasi-successes will be paraded but paradoxically they won't illustrate real policy directions. Confusion is the policy—that, and the enabling of Russian power, the removal of sanctions, and the neutering of NATO.

For the best guide to the garish sensory wallpaper of the Trump

---

* http://www.msnbc.com/msnbc-news/watch/will-reality-intrude-on-reality
-tv-presidency-838025795988.

era's assault on our senses we must look to *Russia Today* (*RT*) and other Russian news media. They pioneered post-fact reality as mainstream culture. Peter Pomeranzev's book *Nothing Is True, Everything Is Possible* studies the phenomenon and lays it out plainly. In essence, the kind of supermarket gossip-tabloid material that once infested our peripheral vision now moves front and center. It is total fantasy—for the masses—every so often containing a tiny germ of truth. Total fantasy, and not even simple lies like Kellyanne Conway's recent assertion that the intelligence services clearly concluded Russia hadn't successfully influenced the election. (They concluded no such thing.) Or Trump's notorious assertion months ago that Mexico's president, after their meeting, had agreed to pay for the border wall. It will feel more like a wholly fabricated unending theater of bizarrerie and Orwellian inversions. As Hirschorn says in the MSNBC interview, we look for the wrong things in Trump's world, such as content and argument. "In reality TV it really isn't about content, it's about show, about performance . . . it's about endless chaos." *

ORWELLIAN INVERSIONS

Turkey's president just celebrated Journalism Day, soberly and without irony. Trump's style hews closer to his postmodern reality show experience. As Michael Hirschorn says, "really great reality TV talent really doesn't know or soon forgets the difference between reality and television." † Trump deploys a sort of loud kitsch with a built-in subliminal wink at the audience: "We both know this is fake, mere performance, but it's a show you're complicit in. That's your level of participation. Leave the rest to me." This echoes the false-real tone of Putin's rule in Russia, where his face carries an almost-smirk in

---

* http://www.msnbc.com/msnbc-news/watch/will-reality-intrude-on-reality
-tv-presidency-838025795988.

† Ibid.

every television appearance. The implied message goes something like: "You and I, all of us, know that this popular display nonsense, this dealing with the public, is a total charade; it never happened during the old KGB days. It's all mere performance to fill the airwaves. The people don't decide anything, not even by their vote; just look at the recent U.S. election. Here's our pact: you stay entertained but confused, paranoid even. That's why you need me."

THE TERRIFYING LESSONS OF THE PHILIPPINES' VIGILANTE PRESIDENT

Peter Apps

(Philippines)

Originally published on Reuters (December 2, 2016)

Every morning in the Philippines, a handful of bodies are found littering the streets. Their faces are often covered in black plastic tape. Sometimes there are signs of torture. Usually, they have been shot in the head. Few bother police—they are usually suspected of being responsible.

No one, frankly, should be surprised that it is happening. The country's democratically elected leader, after all, was elected promising to do just this, cracking down on what he has described as a "drug menace" in the country.

If one world leader exemplifies some of the more alarming trends taking place in politics this decade, it is Filipino president Rodrigo Duterte. His election and the policies he has pursued since entering office represent a comprehensive rejection of decades, if not centuries, of hard-won moves toward respect for human rights and the rule of law.

Such legal niceties, Duterte and those around him argue, have simply given criminals and others too much space. It's the sort of sentiment that has sometimes also found its place in Donald Trump's campaign—the US president-elect talked, after all, of getting "really nasty" against the Islamic State. In the Philippines, however, the death toll is already believed to have run to more than

5,000. Of these, 2,000 were shot in armed confrontations with the police—with 3,000 more suffering extrajudicial executions.

"The number [of drug addicts] is quite staggering and scary," Duterte said in his inaugural State of the Nation address. "I have to slaughter these idiots for destroying my country."

The Filipino leader has been in power barely six months. He has another five and a half years until he next faces a poll.

That his rhetoric can gain traction among voters should not itself be a surprise—the idea of vigilante justice clearly still has an appeal, if only evidenced by the way in which it remains such a common Hollywood theme. As mayor of Davao City for more than two decades, the Filipino president reveled in such imagery—he was often referred to as "the Punisher" or "Duterte Harry," the latter a reference to the cinematic vigilante "Dirty Harry," played by Clint Eastwood.

As mayor, Duterte was repeatedly accused of involvement in death squads targeting both criminals and political enemies. Earlier this year, a man claiming to be a former associate accused the president of taking part in some killings and ordering others, including having a man fed to a crocodile in 2007. Nothing was ever proven, however—and in those days, Duterte denied direct involvement. An official inquiry published at the beginning of this year—and, unsurprisingly, heavily criticized—said it found no evidence of the reported death squad killings or Duterte's own direct involvement.

Since Duterte took the presidency in June, however, he has been much more outspoken—as well as willing to take responsibility for what some estimate could be several thousand deaths. This week, he openly threatened to target human rights activists whom he accused of getting in the way of the purge.

Such tactics appear to have cost the Philippines its long-running alliance with the United States—at least under the presidency of Barack Obama. (The Filipino leader has said he hopes to have a rather better relationship with Trump.) Duterte has talked openly of seeking alliances with Russia and China instead; both countries are seen as more likely to let the Philippines do whatever it wishes when it comes to internal matters.

Duterte is clearly an outlier. For now, however, his approach is serving him relatively well when it comes to Filipino domestic politics—according to one survey, he remains one of the most trusted leaders in Southeast Asia.

But he is also part of a wider trend—one that may well be accelerating. There have always, of course, been leaders who have made a virtue of "doing what it takes" to restore order and have been relatively happy to get a reputation for sometimes brutal tactics, even if they publicly deny them.

Rwandan president Paul Kagame, for example, has always said his country needs to sometimes take a tough line with those who try to destabilize it if Rwanda is to avoid a repeat of the 1994 genocide. Sri Lanka's then-leaders used sometimes brutal measures to end the civil war with Tamil Tiger rebels in 2009. After the chaos of the 1990s, Russian president Vladimir Putin has ruthlessly traded off his reputation for toughness, particularly in the long-running insurgency in Chechnya, where Moscow's forces have long been accused of unrestricted use of force and widespread rights abuses.

Most of those leaders, however, have always sought to deny outright responsibility—or at least maintain a degree of deniability—when it comes to unquestioned acts of extrajudicial murder. By being willing to make it so explicitly a tool of government policy, Duterte has significantly moved the goalposts of what might be deemed to be acceptable in international affairs.

Where he has been criticized, he has been outspoken in his response, even threatening to leave the United Nations and join a new group—perhaps Russian and Chinese-backed—that would also include African governments keen to push back on some international human rights demands. Earlier this year, South Africa and Burundi both announced they would quit the International Criminal Court, set up in response to the genocides of the 1990s, but which critics say has been selective in which conflicts it chooses to investigate.

These trends are also, in some respects at least, clearly evident in the West. Trump talked openly of waterboarding and targeting the families of suspected militants during his campaign, although it remains uncertain whether he will pursue such policies in office. Far-right European political parties and columnists have periodically called for a much tougher approach to migration, suggesting this might sometimes include the use of live ammunition to maintain potentially overwhelmed borders.

What this represents is an unraveling of the rules-based system—and in many respects the essential concept of basic human rights—enshrined in the United Nations charter signed by most progressive nations after World War II.

That commitment was always imperfect—and frequently desperately hypocritically imposed. Still, it has rarely been as pushed back against as it is in the Philippines today.

Next year may well see the forces of Syrian president Bashar al-Assad reassert control in Syria and the unraveling of the unsuccessful US-backed policy of supporting ineffectual opposition fighters. The United States and Europe will likely see a considerable political reaction against what had been seen as relatively fundamental rights, particularly when it comes to asylum and freedom of movement.

None of those things are unnecessarily unreasonable. What the Philippines reminds us, though, is just how short a journey it might be to really tear up some of the most basic rules that had been seen as underpinning a civilized society. Worse still, it can even be popular.

REMARKS ON ERASURE

Ai Weiwei

(China)

Translated by Perry Link, January 19, 2017

Things of this sort happen to me all the time: Within a month, at separate exhibitions in Beijing and Shanghai—once with advance notice to me and once without—my name was blotted out.* Other people might take such treatment in stride, as nothing to get huffy about. Not me. I see the labels on my work as a measure of the value I have produced—like water-level markers at a riverbank. Other people might just shrug, but I can't. I have no illusions, though, that my unwillingness to shrug affects anyone else's willingness to do so.

My art begins with who I am, trying to show in my own small contexts how I get through life. I don't start with a determination to resist anything; I just see what I see and look for ways to show to myself how I am getting through life and how I can measure my relationships with others. This means I need to be authentic. To be otherwise would mean falling into habit and inertia, as if accepting that fate is in one's blood and that being born on a certain piece of ground determines the kind of person one must be.

---

* Editors' note: On April 26, 2014, Ai Weiwei's name and works were removed from 15 Years of Chinese Contemporary Art Award (CCAA), a group show in Shanghai. One month later, the Ullens Center for Contemporary Art in Beijing held the exhibition Hans van Dijk: 5000 Names. Though he had been invited to participate with three works of art, Ai Weiwei's name was omitted from the press release, leading him to remove his artwork from the center.

For people who accept a recumbent position toward authority, "getting by" becomes the supreme value. They smile, bow, and nod their heads, and such performance usually leads to lifestyles that are comfortable, trouble-free, and even cushy. My different approach strikes these people as obtuse. They assume a superiority that they pretend to be based on universally recognized common sense and declare with absolute confidence that the roots of Weiwei's discontent lie in his own appetite for trouble and in his desire to advance his own interests.

This attitude is essentially defensive on their part. It is obvious that, in any dispute, if one side is silenced, the words of the other side will go unrebutted. There is no way to argue an issue toward a reasoned balance. That's what we have here: the self-silenced majority, sycophants of a powerful regime, are resentful of people like me who speak out, and they are doubly bitter because they know that their debasement comes by their own hand. Hence self-defense also becomes self-comfort.

Life in China is saturated with pretense. People pretend ignorance and speak in ambiguities. Nobody asks "What happened?" "How could it happen?" or "Is there no way it could have not happened?" In a place where everything is fake, right down to the last hair, anyone who stands up to quibble about truth seems naïve, even childlike. In the end I find the "naïve" route the only one left open to me. I am as narrow-minded as those narrow-minded Uighurs and Tibetans.

I am not allowed to travel in China and am banned from the state media, where I am regularly scolded (but it matters little, since the scoldings usually don't reach me). Commentators in the state media pretend to be even-handed, but that's impossible, given where they sit, behind the state's protective curtain. They will never debate me one-on-one, and why should they, given the overwhelming advantage that the self-silenced majority gives to them? They don't address topics like rights to free speech or the quality of life for the vast majority of Chinese. Their special expertise is in unscrupulous attack on voices that have already been repressed.

Debate on cultural questions necessarily involves questions of basic values. I do what I can to show cruelties, the subtle and the not so subtle. In China as it is today, rational resistance can be based only on the small actions of individual people.

Everybody in China knows that a censorship system exists, but there is very little discussion of why it exists. The content offered by the Chinese state media, after its processing by political censors, is not free information but information that has been selected, filtered, and assigned its place, inevitably restricting the free and independent will of readers and viewers. At first glance the censorship seems invisible, but its omnipresent washing of people's feelings and perceptions creates limits on the information people receive, select, and rely upon. The placing of limits on knowledge and morals is key to imposing ideological slavery.

The harm of a censorship system is not just that it impoverishes intellectual life; it also fundamentally distorts the rational order in which the natural and spiritual worlds are understood. Censoring speech removes the possibility of freedom in what one chooses to take in and to express to others, and this inevitably leads to depression in people. Judgments become distorted and rationality itself begins to slip away. Group behavior can become wild, abnormal, and violent. Whenever the state controls or blocks information, it not only reasserts the absolute superiority of its power; it also elicits from the people whom it rules a voluntary submission to the system and an acknowledgment of its dominion. This in turn supports the axiom of the debased: Accept dependency in return for practical benefits.

The most elegant way to adjust to censorship is to engage in self-censorship. It is the perfect means for allying with power and setting the stage for the mutual exchange of benefit. Here I do not mean that sacrificing one's own thought and values to a threatening power is a problem only of the weak; in the international system, when foreign countries interact with our rulers, the pursuit of interests (and sometimes the survival of the relationship itself) is seen to require observation of self-censorship. Foreign governments find over time that the wisest course is to accept self-censorship. In any case, the silencing of voices, whether by censorship or by induced self-censorship, is an essential strut for the regime's power.

Censoring speech, and thereby keeping the censored in a position of dependency, is the first principle in maintaining the regime's absolute power. Blocking information and limiting expression in the news, in print publications, in textbooks, on the Internet, and in music concerts or art exhibitions, and subjecting activity at every level to monitoring and limitation, is akin to the pervasive spread of pollution in the air. The censorship system relies on robbing a person of the self-perception that one needs in order to maintain an independent existence. It cuts off life's access to independence and true happiness. Wherever fear dominates, true happiness vanishes and individual will runs dry. Kowtowing to power in exchange for small pleasures may seem minor, but without it, the brutal assault of the censorship system would not be possible.

The system rewards ordinary people for their cooperation automatically; there is no need to compete for the rewards. Managers of cultural projects need to do more than that—they need to show proactively that they "get it" and will accommodate the authoritarians and care for their face. They know that if anything causes unhappiness higher up, a project, and perhaps an organization, is scrubbed. In this kind of system, where works of art rise or fall not in free competition but by corrupt criteria, any creator of art that has any genuine vitality must act dumb and agree to tacit understandings. The rules of the game in fact are as simple as they are primitive: All artists who play the game must acknowledge their original sin, and any bit of brilliance or fanciful display must be doing one of two things: resisting or selling out.

Because the censorship system needs cooperation and tacit

understanding from the censored, I disagree with the common view that the censored are its victims. Voluntary self-censorship brings benefits to a person, and the system would not work if the voluntarism were not there. Darwin would recognize the pattern; its principles are simple and easy to grasp.

Let's look at my own rights of expression. It is well known that I cannot speak in any public forum. My name is expunged everywhere in the public media. My *virtual* existence, if we can call it that, exists only among people who notice me by choice, and those people fall clearly into two categories: those who see my behavior as strengthening the meaning of their lives, and those who see me as obstructing their roads to benefit. Whether the goals of those in the latter group are meant to be morally uplifting or are merely for practical benefit doesn't matter; in both cases my obstruction is the reason they cannot pardon me. Only when China offers fair and just platforms for expression of public opinion will we have ways of meeting minds by using our words. I support the establishment of such platforms. This should be the first principle in making social justice possible.

People who willingly do self-censorship are vulnerable to moral challenges of many kinds. They have never been victims and never will be—despite their occasional show of tear-wiping. Each time they redisplay their acceptance of servility, they bring warmth to the hearts of the authoritarians and do direct harm to people who protest. Their craven stance, when it becomes widespread, becomes the deep reason for the moral collapse of our society. If these people believe that their choice to cooperate is their only way to avoid victimhood, they are embarking on an ill-fated journey in the dark.

An artist is a mover, a political participant. Aesthetic judgment inevitably involves other components of one's worldview, especially ethics and philosophy. Like it or not, ethics and philosophy are inside any true art. It's vain to look for counterexamples, because there are none.

Questions like how to view freedom of expression, how to protect it, and how to maintain independence of viewpoint are simple and clear in their original nature; they are not things that someone can evade with duplicitous language or can rub out of existence at will. Especially in times of historic change, genuine aesthetic values will always have an advantage. A society that persecutes people who persist in cleaving to individual values is an uncivilized society that has no future.

What each person needs to do is only to take responsibility for his or her own value judgments. When a person's values are put on public display, the standards and ethics of that person and, on the other side, of the society as a whole might both undergo challenge. This principle is inherent in my philosophy of art. An individual's free expression can stimulate a more distinctive kind of exchange, and expressions that are more distinctive will in turn lead to more distinctive ways of exchanging views.

The rights that I seek to defend are sharable ones; where I fail, though, the responsibility is mine alone.

Part IV

Latin America

WHAT HUGO CHÁVEZ TELLS US ABOUT DONALD TRUMP

Alberto Barrera Tyszka

(Venezuela)

Originally published in *The New York Times* (September 20, 2016)

MEXICO CITY—Long before becoming president, when he was a soldier, Hugo Chávez organized cultural activities, most notably beauty pageants. On a stage, microphone in hand, Mr. Chávez served as host, pumping up the audience and announcing the winner. The showman in him already struggled to emerge from under the uniform. Mr. Chávez said he imitated the proceedings he had seen on television in these improvised contests. This is how he learned to play to an audience.

When he tried to seize power through a coup d'état years later, in 1992, the resulting media frenzy sent him another sign. His military failure turned into a political victory: When Mr. Chávez appeared on TV to call for his colleagues to give up, he won over the audience. One minute on the screen was more effective than tanks, machine guns, and bullets.

That was the start of his political career. He didn't rise to power through social struggles. He became president without ever holding public office or a representative position that would have required him to negotiate or compromise. From his first election as president, in 1998, to his last one, in 2012—shortly before his death at age fifty-eight in March 2013—Mr. Chávez became an expert in using television as a form of government.

Now Donald J. Trump is proposing the same thing to the United States.

Beyond their ideological differences, Mr. Trump, a populist right-winger, and Mr. Chávez, a leftist strongman, share the same telegenic vocation. They both built a career via television spectacle. Every Sunday, Mr. Chávez appeared on a program called *Aló Presidente,* in which he would sing, talk about current events, or appoint and dismiss ministers—reminiscent of Trump's television catchphrase "You're fired!" There was no time limit for *Aló Presidente.* The longest episode lasted eight hours and seven minutes.

Not only that, but Mr. Chávez could decide to appear at any time through mandatory broadcasts transmitted over all the country's airwaves. By 2012, he had appeared in 2,377 of them, adding up to 1,642 hours. Every day, Mr. Chávez was featured for an average of 54 minutes as the main character of some kind of television broadcast. His true utopia appeared to be the consolidation of a telegovernment.

Mr. Trump's campaign wouldn't be possible without television. Not only because of the coverage, worth hundreds of millions of dollars he has enjoyed, but also because of the reality show *The Apprentice,* on which he was host, judge, and prize. From there he began associating his image with the idea that financial problems could be resolved easily, authoritatively, in one hour of television. His campaign is also like that. To him, democracy is a reality show contest.

Mr. Chávez and Mr. Trump are expert provocateurs. Their narratives are closer to audiovisual fiction than to political debate.

An eloquent example is Mr. Trump's visit with President Enrique Peña Nieto of Mexico. Mr. Trump appeared conciliatory and diplomatic in Mexico City. Hours later, in Phoenix, not only did he say that Mexico would pay 100 percent of the cost of a border wall, but he also unleashed another ferocious attack against immigrants. His coherence depends on the audience. The only thing that matters to him is the emotional effect he has on the people listening and the impact it has in the media.

Even when it comes to reporting on his health, Mr. Trump goes into showman mode. Why does he need to release his medical records if everyone can see him admitting he is overweight on *The Dr. Oz Show*? There is no problem too big to be tackled on TV.

Mr. Chávez also used controversy as bait. He was able to invent or magnify a conflict to keep his audience hanging. He knew perfectly well the power of language. In 2011 he said: "Obama, you are a fraud, a total fraud. If I could be a candidate in the United States, I would sweep the floor with you." These are words that are reminiscent of a reality TV show. Mr. Trump also knows these tricks well and, like Mr. Chávez, has no scruples when it comes to using them. He said of President Obama: "He's the founder of ISIS. He's the founder of ISIS. He's the founder. He founded ISIS."

There is no substance behind these words, just a media fire. Their narrative is also very similar. They both denounce an unfair present and invoke a glorious destiny that has been taken from us by an enemy force.

It's a flattering fantasy, but it's also a dangerous story: It legitimizes violence.

Mr. Chávez's and Mr. Trump's speeches raise the possibility that violence may be the best solution. Mr. Chávez routinely made threats. He always reminded others that his revolution was "peaceful but armed."

Charisma like that of Mr. Chávez or Mr. Trump is also a symptom. It reflects what exists in their own societies. Mr. Chávez emerged in a country that had nurtured the certainty of being rich, although it lived in poverty. Mr. Trump speaks to Americans who are suffering the consequences of an economic crisis and globalization, who see their country as being contaminated by Latin Americans and Muslims.

Mr. Trump and Mr. Chávez spread the idea that social problems have easy and quick resolutions. They represent the mirage of magical solutions and the triumph of television over politics.

In Venezuela, the consequences of having opted for a media

demagogue are evident in Mr. Chávez's legacy: Inflation forecasts for 2016 exceed 700 percent. Almost two million Venezuelans have been forced to migrate. The country is on the verge of a humanitarian crisis. Voting for Chávez meant voting for the destruction of the country.

Like Mr. Chávez, Donald Trump used to organize beauty pageants. Like him, he may get a chance to remake a country.

The complexity of United States politics would make Mr. Trump's journey to destruction more difficult. But Mr. Chávez's parable is also a cautionary tale about voters' vulnerability to the spell of charisma and media banality.

IN VENEZUELA, WE COULDN'T STOP CHÁVEZ. DON'T MAKE THE SAME MISTAKES WE DID

Andrés Miguel Rondón

(Venezuela)

Originally published in *The Washington Post* (January 27, 2017)

How to let a populist beat you, over and over again.

Donald Trump is an avowed capitalist; Hugo Chávez was a socialist with communist dreams. One builds skyscrapers, the other expropriated them. But politics is only one-half policy: The other, darker half is rhetoric. Sometimes the rhetoric takes over. Such has been our lot in Venezuela for the past two decades—and such is yours now, Americans. Because in one regard, Trump and Chávez are identical. They are both masters of populism.

The recipe for populism is universal. Find a wound common to many, find someone to blame for it, and make up a good story to tell. Mix it all together. Tell the wounded you know how they feel. That you found the bad guys. Label them: the minorities, the politicians, the businessmen. Caricature them. As vermin, evil masterminds, haters and losers, you name it. Then paint yourself as the savior. Capture the people's imagination. Forget about policies and plans, just enrapture them with a tale. One that starts with anger and ends in vengeance. A vengeance they can participate in.

That's how it becomes a movement. There's something soothing in all that anger. Populism is built on the irresistible allure of simplicity. The narcotic of the simple answer to an intractable question. The problem is now made simple.

The problem is you.

How do I know? Because I grew up as the "you" Trump is about to turn you into. In Venezuela, the urban middle class I come from was cast as the enemy in the political struggle that followed Chávez's arrival in 1998. For years I watched in frustration as the opposition failed to do anything about the catastrophe overtaking our nation. Only later did I realize that this failure was self-inflicted. So now, to my American friends, here is some advice on how to avoid Venezuela's mistakes.

Don't forget who the enemy is.

Populism can survive only amid polarization. It works through the unending vilification of a cartoonish enemy. Never forget that you're that enemy. Trump needs you to be the enemy, just like all religions need a demon. A scapegoat. "But facts!" you'll say, missing the point entirely.

What makes you the enemy? It's very simple to a populist: If you're not a victim, you're a culprit.

During the 2007 student-led protests against the government's closure of RCTV, then the second-biggest TV channel in Venezuela, Chávez continually went on air to frame us students as "pups of the American Empire," "supporters of the enemy of the country"— spoiled, unpatriotic babies who only wanted to watch soap operas. Using our socioeconomic background as his main accusation, he sought to frame us as the direct inheritors of the mostly imagined "oligarchs" of our fathers' generation. The students who supported Chavismo were "children of the homeland," "sons of the people," "the future of the country." Not for one moment did the government's analysis go beyond such cartoons.

The problem is not the message but the messenger, and if you don't realize this, you will be wasting your time.

Show no contempt.

Don't feed polarization, disarm it. This means leaving the theater of injured decency behind.

That includes rebukes such as the one the *Hamilton* cast gave Vice President–elect Mike Pence shortly after the election. While sincere, it only antagonized Trump; it surely did not convince a single Trump supporter to change his or her mind. Shaming has never been an effective method of persuasion.

The Venezuelan opposition struggled for years to get this. We wouldn't stop pontificating about how stupid Chavismo was, not only to international friends but also to Chávez's electoral base. "Really, this guy? Are you nuts? You must be nuts," we'd say.

The subtext was clear: Look, idiots—he will destroy the country. He's blatantly siding with the bad guys: Fidel Castro, Vladimir Putin, the white supremacists, or the guerrillas. He's not that smart. He's threatening to destroy the economy. He has no respect for democracy or for the experts who work hard and know how to do business.

I heard so many variations on these comments growing up that my political awakening was set off by the tectonic realization that Chávez, however evil, was not actually stupid.

Neither is Trump: Getting to the highest office in the world requires not only sheer force of will but also great, calculated rhetorical precision. The kind only a few political geniuses are born with and one he flamboyantly brandishes.

"We are in a rigged system, and a big part of the rigging are these dishonest people in the media," Trump said late in the campaign, when he was sounding the most like Chávez. "Isn't it amazing? They don't even want to look at you folks." The natural conclusion is all too clear: Turn off the TV, just listen to me. The constant boos at his rallies only confirmed as much. By looking down on Trump's supporters, you've lost the first battle. Instead of fighting polarization, you've played into it.

The worst you can do is bundle moderates and extremists together and think that America is divided between racists and liberals. That's the textbook definition of polarization. We thought our country was split between treacherous oligarchs and Chávez's uneducated, gullible base. The only one who benefited was Chávez.

Don't try to force him out.

Our opposition tried every single trick in the book. Coup d'état? Check. Ruinous oil strike? Check. Boycotting elections in hopes that international observers would intervene? You guessed it.

Look, opponents were desperate. We were right to be. But a hissy fit is not a strategy.

The people on the other side—and crucially, independents—will rebel against you if you look like you're losing your mind. You will have proved yourself to be the very thing you're claiming to be fighting against: an enemy of democracy. And all the while you're giving the populist and his followers enough rhetorical fuel to rightly call you a saboteur, an unpatriotic schemer, for years to come.

To a big chunk of the population, the Venezuelan opposition is still that spoiled, unpatriotic schemer. It sapped the opposition's effectiveness for the years when we'd need it most.

Clearly, the United States has much stronger institutions and a fairer balance of powers than Venezuela. Even out of power, Democrats have no apparent desire to try anything like a coup. Which is good. Attempting to force Trump out, rather than digging in to fight his agenda, would just distract the public from whatever failed policies the administration is making. In Venezuela, the opposition focused on trying to reject the dictator by any means possible—when we should have just kept pointing out how badly Chávez's rule was hurting the very people he claimed to be serving.

Find a counterargument. (No, not the one you think.)

Don't waste your time trying to prove that this grand idea is better than that one. Ditch all the big words. The problem, remember, is not the message but the messenger. It's not that Trump supporters are too stupid to see right from wrong; it's that you're more valuable to them as an enemy than as a compatriot. Your challenge is to prove that you belong in the same tribe as them—that you are American in exactly the same way they are.

In Venezuela, we fell into this trap in a bad way. We wrote again and again about principles, about separation of powers, civil liberties, the role of the military in politics, corruption, and economic policy. But it took opposition leaders ten years to figure out that they needed to actually go to the slums and the countryside. Not for a speech or a rally, but for a game of dominoes or to dance salsa—to show they were Venezuelans, too, that they weren't just dour scolds and could hit a baseball, could tell a joke that landed. That they could break the tribal divide, come down off the billboards and show that they were real. This is not populism by other means. It is the only way of establishing your standing. It's deciding not to live in an echo chamber. To press pause on the siren song of polarization.

Because if the music keeps going, yes—you will see neighbors deported and friends of different creeds and sexual orientations living in fear and anxiety, your country's economic inequality deepening along the way. But something worse could happen. In Venezuela, whole generations were split in two. A sense of shared culture was wiped out. Rhetoric took over our history books, our future, our own sense of self. We lost the freedom to be anything larger than cartoons.

This does not have to be your fate. You can be different. Recognize that you're the enemy Trump requires. Show concern, not contempt, for the wounds of those who brought him to power. By all means, be patient with democracy and struggle relentlessly to free yourself from the shackles of the caricature the populists have drawn of you.

It's a tall order. But the alternative is worse. Trust me.

WILL DEMOCRACY SURVIVE TRUMP'S POPULISM? LATIN AMERICA MAY TELL US

Carlos de la Torre

(Latin America)

Originally published in *The New York Times* (December 15, 2016)

LEXINGTON, Ky.—Will Donald J. Trump follow the populist script for concentrating power by cracking down on critics? Or are the foundations of American democracy and the institutions of civil society strong enough to resist such an action? For answers, Americans should take a look at Latin America, where, starting in the 1940s, elected populists undermined democracy.

Populism is not an ideology but a strategy to get to power and to govern. Two of Latin America's most influential populists, Juan Perón of Argentina and Hugo Chávez of Venezuela, saw politics as a Manichaean confrontation between two antagonistic camps, just as Mr. Trump does. In their view, they did not face political rivals, but enemies who needed to be destroyed.

Populist leaders tend to present themselves as extraordinary characters whose mission is to liberate the people. To get elected they politicize feelings of fear or resentment. Once in government, they attack the liberal constitutional framework of democracy, which they view as constraining the will of the people. Populists are profoundly antipluralist and claim that they embody the people as a whole. Chávez boasted, "This is not about Hugo Chávez; this is about a people." Similarly, Mr. Trump said at a rally in Florida:

"It's not about me—it's about all of you. It's about all of us, together as a country."

The terms *people* and *elite* are vague. The "people" of Perón and Chávez were the downtrodden, and the nonwhite. Mr. Trump's "people" are white, mostly Christian citizens who produce wealth and do not live on government handouts. The enemies of Chávez and Perón were corrupt politicians, foreign-oriented economic elites, imperialism, and the privately owned news media. In Mr. Trump's presidential campaign, Mexicans were cast as the anti-American other, and Muslims depicted as potential terrorists whose values are contrary to American Christianity. He painted African-Americans as delinquents or as victims living in conditions of alienation and despair. Mr. Trump's enemies were also the news media, companies and countries that profit from globalization, and liberal elites that defend political correctness.

Populists make their own rules for the political game, and part of their strategy is to manipulate the news media. Chávez and Rafael Correa, Ecuador's populist president, blurred the lines between entertainment and news, using their own weekly TV shows to announce major policies, attack the opposition, sing popular songs, and, naturally, fire people. They were always on Twitter confronting enemies, and television programs showcased their outrageous words and actions to increase ratings. Mr. Trump might follow these examples and transform debates on issues of national interest into reality TV shows.

Since Latin America's populists feel threatened by those who question their claim to be the embodiment of their people's aspirations, they go after the press. Perón and Chávez nationalized news outlets that criticized them; Alberto Fujimori of Peru used tabloids to smear critics; Mr. Correa has used the legal system to impose astronomical fines on journalists and news media owners. *Diario Hoy,* a center-left newspaper in Ecuador at which I was a columnist, was forced out of business for criticizing the government. Like many journalists and intellectuals in Ecuador, I became a target of the president, who insulted me twice on his national TV show.

Like his Latin American populist cousins, Mr. Trump shows contempt for the news media. He has threatened newspapers and journalists with libel suits. While he has softened his attacks on the news media since the election, a confrontation with watchdog journalists seems inevitable.

Latin American populists also attack civil society. Similarly, Mr. Trump has used harsh language against civil rights groups like Black Lives Matter. Some of his close collaborators are talking about reviving the Committee on Un-American Activities. His support of mass deportations, the use of stop-and-frisk in black and Latino neighborhoods, surveillance of American Muslims, and the rolling back of rights for women and LGBT people could also lead to confrontations with civil and human rights organizations.

Latin American populists do not respect constitutional arrangements like the separation of powers. They attempt to control the judiciary, to take over all watchdog institutions, and to create parties based on the unconditional loyalty to a leader. When leaders come to power amid crises, as when Chávez and Mr. Correa were elected, they can grab power and establish authoritarianism at the expense of democracy. In Argentina, stronger democratic institutions resisted Cristina Fernández de Kirchner's strategy of populist polarization, blocking a change to the Argentine constitution that would have allowed her to stay in power for another term.

The United States has a tradition of checks and balances to control political power. The Constitution divides power into three branches; elections are spaced; power is split between the states and the federal government; and there are two dominant parties. Under these restraints and until Mr. Trump's election, populism was confined to the fringes of the political system. Mr. Trump's populism under this institutional framework would be no more than a passing phase, and the American democracy and civil society would be strong enough to survive populist challenges without major desta-bilizing consequences.

But, even if the institutional framework of democracy does not collapse under Mr. Trump, he has already damaged the democratic public sphere. Hate speech and the denigration of minorities are replacing the politics of cultural recognition and tolerance built by the struggles of feminists and antiracist social movements since the 1960s.

Mr. Trump is a type of political animal unknown to Americans, a far-right populist autocrat. Sexism, racism, and xenophobia got him elected. As president, he will have the authority to expel the groups that he campaigned against. Once in power he will continue to attack the news media, liberal and cosmopolitan elites, and any other groups that challenge his policies.

Democracy is not immune to populist autocrats. Populist polar-ization, attacks on civil rights, and the confrontation with the press could lead in the United States, as in Venezuela and Ecuador, to au-thoritarianism. Chávez and Mr. Correa did not eradicate democracy with a coup d'état. Rather, they slowly strangled democracy by at-tacking civil liberties, regulating the public sphere, and using the legal system to silence critics. Americans who value an inclusive, tolerant, and pluralist country need to be on guard against Trump's following in their footsteps.

NOW, AMERICA, YOU KNOW
HOW CHILEANS FELT

Ariel Dorfman

(Chile)

Originally published in *The New York Times* (December 16, 2016)

DURHAM, N.C.—It is familiar, the outrage and alarm that many Americans are feeling at reports that Russia, according to a secret intelligence assessment, interfered in the United States election to help Donald J. Trump become president.

I have been through this before, overwhelmed by a similar outrage and alarm.

To be specific: On the morning of October 22, 1970, in what was then my home in Santiago de Chile, my wife, Angélica, and I listened to a news flash on the radio. Gen. René Schneider, the head of Chile's armed forces, had been shot by a commando on a street of the capital. He was not expected to survive.

Angélica and I had the same automatic reaction: It's the CIA, we said, almost in unison. We had no proof at the time—though evidence that we were right would eventually (and abundantly) surface—but we did not doubt that this was one more American attempt to subvert the will of the Chilean people.

Six weeks earlier, Salvador Allende, a democratic Socialist, had won the presidency in a free and fair election, in spite of the United States spending millions of dollars on psychological warfare and misinformation to prevent his victory (we'd call it "fake news" today). Allende had campaigned on a program of social and economic justice, and we knew that the government of President Richard M.

Nixon, allied with Chile's oligarchs, would do everything it could to stop Allende's nonviolent revolution from gaining power.

The country was rife with rumors of a possible coup. It had happened in Guatemala and Iran, in Indonesia and Brazil, where leaders opposed to United States interests had been ousted; now it was Chile's turn. That was why General Schneider was assassinated. Because, having sworn loyalty to the Constitution, he stubbornly stood in the way of those destabilization plans.

General Schneider's death did not block Allende's inauguration, but American intelligence services, at the behest of Henry A. Kissinger, continued to assail our sovereignty during the next three years, sabotaging our prosperity ("make the economy scream," Nixon ordered) and fostering military unrest. Finally, on September 11, 1973, Allende was overthrown and replaced by a vicious dictatorship that lasted nearly 17 years. Years of torture and executions and disappearances and exile.

Given all that pain, one might presume that some glee on my part would be justified at the sight of Americans squirming in indignation at the spectacle of their democracy subjected to foreign interference—as Chile's democracy, among many others, was by America. And yes, it is ironic that the CIA—the very agency that cared not a whit for the independence of other nations—is now crying foul because its tactics have been imitated by a powerful international rival.

I can savor the irony, but I feel no glee. This is not only because, as an American citizen myself now, I am once again a victim of this sort of nefarious meddling. My dismay goes deeper than that personal sense of vulnerability. This is a collective disaster: Those who vote in the United States should not have to suffer what those of us who voted in Chile had to go through. Nothing warrants that citizens anywhere should have their destiny manipulated by forces outside the land they inhabit.

The seriousness of this violation of the people's will must not be flippantly underestimated or disparaged.

When Mr. Trump denies, as do his acolytes, the claims by the intelligence community that the election was, in fact, rigged in his favor by a foreign power, he is bizarrely echoing the very responses that so many Chileans got in the early '70s when we accused the CIA of illegal interventions in our internal affairs. He is using now the same terms of scorn we heard back then: Those allegations, he says, are "ridiculous" and mere "conspiracy theory," because it is "impossible to know" who was behind it.

In Chile, we did find out who was "behind it." Thanks to the Church Committee and its valiant, bipartisan 1976 report, the world discovered the many crimes the CIA had been committing, the multiple ways in which it had destroyed democracy elsewhere—in order, supposedly, to save the world from Communism.

This country deserves, as all countries do—including Russia, of course—the possibility of choosing its leaders without someone in a remote room abroad determining the outcome of that election. This principle of peaceful coexistence and respect is the bedrock of freedom and self-determination, a principle that, yet again, has been compromised—this time, with the United States as its victim.

What to do, then, to restore faith in the democratic process?

First, there should be an independent, transparent, and thorough public investigation so that any collusion between American citizens and foreigners bent on mischief can be exposed and punished, no matter how powerful these operatives may be. The president-elect should be demanding such an inquiry, rather than mocking its grounds. The legitimacy of his rule, already damaged by his significant loss in the popular vote, depends on it.

But there is another mission, a loftier one, that the American people, not politicians or intelligence agents, must carry out. The implications of this deplorable affair should lead to an incessant and unforgiving meditation on our shared country, its values, its beliefs, its history.

The United States cannot in good faith decry what has been done to its decent citizens until it is ready to face what it did so often to the equally decent citizens of other nations. And it must firmly resolve never to engage in such imperious activities again.

If ever there was a time for America to look at itself in the mirror, if ever there was a time of reckoning and accountability, it is now.

LATIN AMERICAN REVOLUTIONARIES HAVE SOME URGENT ADVICE FOR DEALING WITH TRUMP

Tim Rogers

(Latin America)

Originally published in *Fusion* (December 14, 2016)

Latin American revolutionaries have some battle-tested advice for how to deal with Donald Trump: *Get organized. Get connected. Get ready to take the fight to him.*

Times and circumstances change, but authoritarianism looks eerily similar throughout history, as Umberto Eco points out in his seminal essay on eternal fascism. The rise of Trump is a movie Latin Americans have seen before. And if you think the previews and the casting suck, just wait until the ending.

Even before he takes office, Trump is already acting the part of a banana republic *caudillo*—one who uses Twitter instead of a palace balcony to make crazy proclamations.

He's a boorish anti-intellectual who bullies women and union leaders, threatens immigrants and religious minorities, rails against the free press, blurs personal business and politics, is shameless about nepotism and cronyism, has murky ties to the Kremlin, is narcissistic despite looking like a Muppet monster, and is so garish and gaudy he makes Muammar Gaddafi look subtle. Dress Trump in olive drab, dark sunglasses, and a fake beard and he could star in a remake of the Woody Allen film *Bananas*.

But what looks like a Latin Americanization of US democracy could be a golden opportunity to reinvigorate grassroots activism.

It's a chance for America's rusty left to form new alliances, articulate a modern agenda for social justice, and imbue a younger generation with a deep awareness of human rights. It won't be easy, but it might just be the kick in the pants that this country needs.

Although nobody I spoke with is advocating violent insurrection in the United States, those who have led revolutionary movements in Latin America think some of the same principles they applied in clandestine circumstances against tin-pot tyrants could now apply just as well to a peaceful resistance against El Trompudo.

STEP 1: DON'T DEMOBILIZE. ORGANIZE AND GROW.

Former Nicaraguan guerrilla commander Hugo Torres says the first mistake anti-Trump forces could make would be to disperse now that the election is over. The groups that mobilized against Trump's campaign—an opposition that, numerically, is larger than the group who voted for the guy—need to keep the pot boiling once he takes office.

"This wasn't a typical election where only the presidency was in play," says Comandante Uno, who helped lead the Sandinistas' takeover of the National Palace in 1978. "Those who feel disillusioned with the results, and even those who didn't vote, need to organize if they fear that all the advancements that have been achieved over the years are now at risk."

Torres thinks the anti-Trump movement could start to peel away at the president's voter base once he's in office and proves he can't deliver on campaign promises of job growth and economic expansion. Torres predicts others will turn on Trump once they realize his policy aims—including the repeal of Obamacare—hurt the working class even more.

The opposition needs to remember that today's Trump supporters could become valuable anti-Trump allies in the near future, the former rebel leader stressed. So remain vigilant, but don't write them off as the enemy because Trump is probably in his finest hour. Once he's in office, it's a different ball game because the Trumpistas "are no longer going to be content with discourse alone," Torres said.

"Economic growth will be crucial," he said. "The hope these people have in Trump is so great it will only be matched by the size of their deception if Trump doesn't deliver quickly. That's Trump's boomerang."

In the meantime, the rise of Trump provides a valuable opportunity for US activists to look beyond their borders and form a stronger nexus with international rights movements, says Salvadoran feminist leader Vilma Vasquez.

"This might be the best opportunity we have had for a North–South dialogue between the US and Latin America," Vasquez said. "We have wanted this for years. Collective action is the only way forward."

STEP 2: USE CLEAR LANGUAGE AND TAILOR MESSAGES FOR DIFFERENT GROUPS.

Trump's campaign was successful in part because his messaging is so simple: Drain the swamp! Build the wall! Lock her up! Make America Great Again!

The opposition can learn from that. Simple messaging and clear labeling are powerful tools in the age of Twitter.

"You have to call things by their name: fascism. And a united front will stop it," says Henry Ruiz, the Sandinista guerrilla hero known as Modesto.

Targeted messaging is also important, says former Salvadoran rebel commander Guadalupe Martinez. It's a mistake to think that all Latinos are allies in the fight for immigration reform, or that political opponents to Trump are necessarily interested in social justice issues. Messages need to be tailored to "awaken consciousness" in different groups and "mobilize" everyone toward the same goal, Martinez says.

"Political groups understand a political message, while groups working on solidarity issues respond more to messages that focus on ethics and morality," Martinez told me.

Social media should be used to target different groups with different messages, she says, because "a good message can get massive circulation."

Allies can then be brought together under a common cause, Modesto says.

"Why not raise a banner in defense of the popular vote?" the former Sandinista guerrilla told me. "Hillary would have beaten Trump. Gore would have beaten Bush. So why can't that be a common cause for the opposition? A call for the United States' democracy to function like others?"

STEP 3: STAY ON THE OFFENSIVE. DON'T GIVE AN INCH.

There's a principle of revolution known as the strategic offensive, the idea that the best defense is a good offense. It's a strategy that Central American rebel movements used when fighting dictatorships, but it also applies to organizing social movements against any populist demagogue, revolutionaries say.

"You need to establish coordination between all sectors participating in the movement, but do so in a way that's offensive and not defensive," says former FMLN revolutionary Sonia Umanzor. "We can't wait for them to strike us to react."

Trump is always on the offensive. If social movements (and the press, for that matter) continue to react to each of his midnight Twitter attacks, they'll always be off-balance while Trump continues to move the chains. The best way to deal with him is with a counteroffensive—take the fight to him, force him to react, keep him off his game.

Honduran indigenous activist Laura Zúñiga Cáceres says the

best way to challenge power is with clear proposals that offer "a different vision" for the country. "When we have clear goals, we will move beyond a defensive position," she says.

The most important thing is to not stop fighting, says Chile's Lautaro Guanca. "People who fight, win. People who don't, don't. People who fight advance. People who don't, don't."

Part V

Journalists on Covering Trump

Editors' note: Of the many challenges the Trump administration poses to American democracy, the pressures faced by journalists and the media are uniquely troubling. In this special section, journalists from South Africa and Russia to Toronto and Washington, D.C., reflect on how the Fourth Estate can most effectively operate in the era of Trump and serve as a constitutionally protected check on government power.

AFRICAN JOURNALISTS HAVE TIPS FOR THEIR US COUNTERPARTS ON DEALING WITH A PRESIDENT THAT HATES THE PRESS

Mohamed Keita

(Africa)

Originally published in *Quartz Africa* (December 7, 2016)

Last week, *Washington Post* executive editor Marty Baron voiced great apprehension about press freedom in the United States under a Donald Trump presidency. "Many journalists wonder with considerable weariness what it is going to be like for us during the next four [years]," Baron said in a stirring speech. "Will we be incessantly harassed and vilified? Will the new administration seize on opportunities to try intimidating us? Will we face obstruction at every turn?"

As America enters the era of a thin-skinned president known for lashing out at press coverage that does not meet his approval, it might be helpful for US news media to draw from the experiences of journalists operating in hostile environments. Many of such environments are in Africa, particularly those countries with long-serving presidents who have been in power for decades.

"There's a thin line between objective critique of the state with regard to security and being called unpatriotic, a terrorist sympathizer."

Ugandan journalist Angelo Izama, a former Knight Fellow at Stanford University, commented with sarcasm on the peculiar situation of US journalists. "I was joking with Charles Onyango Obbo [another Ugandan journalist] about being consultants to American journalists who may now face similar challenges with the advent of the African leader Donald Trump." Izama was probably riffing off Trevor Noah's comic but profound observation that Donald Trump is just like an African president.

One has to only consider the fact that the only other world leader with a habit of snapping at journalists and other critics with angry tweets is Rwanda's Paul Kagame. The direct comparison between Trump and Kagame probably stops there, but one could also find similarities—in terms of vilification of the press—between Trump and the Gambia's outgoing Yahya Jammeh or Uganda's Yoweri Museveni.

"From the outside looking in, I am kind of feeling bad for journalists under a Trump administration," said Liberian editor Rodney Sieh, who has worked for several US newspapers including the *Kansas City Star* and the *Post Standard* in Syracuse, New York. "It is clear to see that American journalists are in for a very tough roller-coaster ride."

Sieh, Izama, and other journalists from the around the continent carry many bruises from political intimidation. "Initially, for me, it was shocking," said Kenyan investigative journalist John-Allan Namu. "The experience showed me just how thin the line is between objective critique of the state with regard to security and being called unpatriotic, a terrorist sympathizer or, very plainly, a terrorist."

The effect of such pressure can be demoralizing. "It took a lot of self-convincing to keep on reporting," he said. "It does make you doubt yourself," according to Sieh. "It is the only way they think they can break you and it can be psychologically draining at times and takes a toll on you as a journalist and [can] make you doubt who or what you are."

Award-winning Angolan investigative journalist Rafael Marques de Morais described the emotional battering. "Psychologically, they make you feel first like you are out of line, then out of touch, then being a nuisance," he said. "For women, they use the weapon of denigration on the basis of sex," said award-winning editor Solange Lusiku of the Congolese newspaper *Le Souverain*. The result can be social ostracism. "My life has been about attending functions and national events and finding myself among people who would rather not speak to me," said editor Bheki Makhubu of Swaziland's the *Nation*.

Intimidation does not stop there. "They start going after you with threats, surrounding you, engaging in backroom deals with your boss to make you feel you are the one out of sync. Then, the lawsuits, the bruisings, the exclusion from official coverage, from official sites," according to Marques, speaking from experience. "There are the pressures on your loved ones, which are unbearable," added Burkinabe journalist Ahmed Newton Barry. "We very quickly realize that our work and life are inseparable," said award-winning Burundian editor Bob Rugurika.

For Izama, the real goal of political intimidation of one journalist or one news organization is to silence others into toeing the line. "Perhaps [. . .] Mr. Trump know this well. If you focus the laser on one person, one organization, it has a great impact on the rest. It isolates and amplifies fear." Intimidation can also lead to self-censorship, according to Ndebele, but it doesn't have to be that way.

For Izama, pressure can bring focus. "Not all fear is bad. The sense of urgency of fear, its psychological pressure has the effect of clarifying why journalism matters," he said, adding: "Because if it were not so important it would not attract the threats it does." In fact, conviction is really important. "What drives you is the need to tell the story," said Zimbabwean journalist Zenzele Ndebele. "There are times when you just don't care what will happen to you when you have written the story as long the story is worthy to be told." Marques put it best: "This is a fight and one shall not have the pretense of neutrality," he said. "In the end it is a fight for one to live quietly in your own country without having to turn a blind eye."

MANEUVERING A NEW REALITY FOR US JOURNALISM

Nic Dawes

(South Africa and India)

Originally published in *Columbia Journalism Review**
(November 22, 2016)

DEAR FRIENDS IN AMERICAN JOURNALISM,

Ordinarily, it is you who offer the rest of the world advice about press freedom, and the accountability architecture of democratic societies, so I understand that it may be strange to hear it coming back at you, but this will not be the last inversion that the election of Donald Trump delivers.

You have some deep resources to draw on for the battle that is closing around you. For starters there is your Constitution, which offers stronger protections than just about any comparable legal framework. And your money, greatly diminished, and unevenly distributed to be sure, but orders of magnitude more plentiful than what your counterparts elsewhere have to call upon. You also have reserves of talent, creativity, and commitment far larger than you are given credit for by your critics, and right now by angry, bewildered, and wounded friends.

But one thing you don't have is experience of what to do when things start to get genuinely bad.

Take it from those of us who have worked in places where the

*www.cjr.org. For information on becoming a member of CJR, please go to http://www.cjr.org/join/membership.php?ad=700-1-join.

institutional fabric is thinner, the legal protections less absolute, and the social license to operate less secure. Not outright dictatorships, but majoritarian democracies where big men—and they are usually men—polish their image in the mirror of state media or social media, while slowly squeezing the life out of independent institutions.

When Donald Trump ditched his press pool twice within days of being elected, and launched a series of Twitter attacks on the *New York Times,* a lot of you sounded surprised. As if you expected him to become a different person once the anointing oil of the Electoral College had touched his brow. Of course there was nothing surprising about his conduct. Rule number 1 of surviving autocracy, as Masha Gessen reminds us, is "Believe the Autocrat." *

When Mr. Trump threatened during the campaign to review America's libel law framework, he was setting out his stall, not bluffing. When he threatened to sue, when he mocked a disabled reporter, when he made clear his affinity for Vladimir Putin and Peter Thiel, he was issuing a warning.

Of course, not being surprised doesn't mean you shouldn't be outraged. As Gessen also wrote, to survive autocracy you have to preserve outrage, and your free press is a beautiful, important thing, even when it is besieged and bedraggled. Perhaps especially then.

The rest of us get irritated with you at times, in the manner of less privileged relatives, but you have given the rest of us a good deal over the years, standards to aspire to, innovation to build on, voices of great clarity. Here is some advice in return, mostly from India and South Africa, where an ostensibly free press is confronted with regulatory, economic, and political pressures that come with majoritarianism.

---

* http://www.nybooks.com/daily/2016/11/10/trump-election-autocracy-rules -for-survival/.

1. Get used to the end of access as you know it.

The president-elect loves to see himself on magazine covers. Don't kid yourself that this means you will enjoy meaningful access to his administration on the terms you are familiar with. There will be a lot less trading of micro-scoops for favorable coverage, the transactional stock in trade of capital city reporting everywhere. In India, for example, after Narendra Modi took power, journalists were banned from government offices they had once wandered freely. They were kicked off the presidential plane. Modi granted no interviews to the domestic press for more than a year. His ministers and senior officials whispered privately that they had been ordered not to speak to the press.

Losing this kind of access isn't all bad. It reminds you that your job is to hold power to account, rather than to join its club. Outsider status can be bracing. But it comes with the choking off of other kinds. Twitter and Instagram posts substitute for the tough back-and-forth of press conferences, officials stonewall legitimate queries, and you wait to publish, because right of reply matters, accuracy matters to you. Not to them.

So you take to the law. But freedom of information filings will be slowed-walked to death or irrelevance, as they increasingly are in India, and other countries where the first flush of enthusiasm over FOIA legislation has been replaced with a deepening chill.

In one case I was involved in in South Africa, three presidents fought us over seven years and two trips to the constitutional court before we won. By then it was too late to do anything but prove a point.

So you have to cultivate other ways to get the data that you need and the democratic process demands.

There are going to be plenty of officials who are deeply uncomfortable with the direction of the administration. Some of them are your sources already, no doubt. But you will need them much more. Especially the awkward squad. The midlevel career bureaucrats, the ones deep down the cc list, the ones who may not have the press secretary's ear, or the inside scoop on how many almonds the president eats at night.

And you are going to need a knowledge of strong encryption if you are going to keep them safe under a regime that has the most sophisticated surveillance capabilities ever imagined, and a president-elect with a history of vindictiveness.

You might think the worst of access culture is already over in Washington. We've seen the videos from the White House correspondents' dinner. It really isn't.

So it will feel strange, this new world. It cuts to your sense of who you are, the proximity to power and the capacity for actual influence that make up for your shitty paycheck and the trolls all over your timeline, but on balance, it is a more honest place, and it is the only one available.

2. Get used to spending more time in court.
You are going to need to litigate to get access to information, but you are also going to have to defend, a lot. Some of the attacks will come from proxies suing over your reporting on corruption, conflicts of interest, and general sleaze. We never lost a suit like that during my time in South Africa, and there were plenty, but we burned countless hours and money we really didn't have, both of which would have been better spent on more reporting.

In India, where the protections are weaker, obscure activists in country towns launch suits against reporters, editors, and proprietors routinely, seeking immense damages in the overburdened and sometimes compromised provincial courts. Anyone who has worked in an Indian newsroom can describe for you what the words "chilling effect" really mean.

You obviously can't back down in the face of these efforts, but you can use them as crusading opportunities, both spreading the story and popularizing your sense of mission. You should be quite unembarrassed about this. You should probably also think about some kind of pooled legal defense fund for smaller outlets.

Much more frightening, of course, are the moments when the proxies step aside and the full might of the security establishment is brought to bear. Your Espionage Act is a truly terrible piece of legislation. Some kind of elite consensus has spared reporters and editors its full force since 1917, but word is the elite consensus is over.

Being fingerprinted for journalism is a very strange experience; you don't want it to become a normal one.

3. Get used to being stigmatized as "opposition."

Trump was quick out of the blocks on this one with his "professional protesters incited by the media" tweet. His subsequent attacks on the *Times* hit a familiar pattern: Call out one prominent enemy *pour encourager les autres,* and let the trolls do the rest. This will escalate. The basic idea is simple: to delegitimize accountability journalism by framing it as partisan.

In South Africa linking the press with the opposition was a routine trope; on really bad days ruling party figures would add the CIA or foreign capitalists.

A member of parliament once asked me, during hearings on a draconian new intelligence law that the national editors' body objected to, "Tell me, are you still South African when you go home at night?"

Narendra Modi, on the other hand, never names his enemies, but the liberal-leaning NDTV carries the brunt of his ire, with one of its channels recently ordered to go off air for a day as punishment for allegedly compromising security with its coverage of a militant attack. And his ardent social media fans do much of the work for him. Steel yourself and take a look at Barkha Dutt's mentions sometime to see the Indian version of Steven Bannon's white nationalist horde.

"Paid media," "presstitutes," "Lutyens journalists" (the equivalent of Beltway insiders) are all routine slurs from India's ruling party, meant to associate the press with the old, corrupt elite and the opposition Congress Party.

The frustrating thing about this approach is that it works quite well, and it is going to work *really* well in America next year.

Why should anyone care about your investigation of the president's conflicts of interest, or his tax bills, if they emanate from the political opposition? The scariest thing about "fake news" is that all news becomes fake. Yours, too.

The challenge is to maintain a tough, independent, journalistic politics, a politics of accountability, equity, and the rule of law without straightforwardly aligning with the partisan opposition. In places like Venezuela, where private media have been forced into a purely oppositional stance, the result has been a shrinking of real spaces for dissent and accountability.

This is a tough line to walk, because people on both sides of the political divide actually want you to fail at it. But it is among your most important tasks.

4. When they can't regulate you away, they will try to buy you out or suck up your oxygen.

Congressional funding for public broadcasting is limited here, as is its audience, so one avenue of media capture is foreclosed. But crony billionaires will be lurking all around the fringes of a distressed industry, happy to tolerate losses in return for a voice. India has hundreds of loss-making TV channels and newspapers. In South Africa, the main English language daily group has been bought out by a presidential crony and gutted. But you can look closer to home for examples, perhaps to Las Vegas.

Some media owners, already ensconced, will tack to the prevailing wind. Gently at first, so you hardly notice it. Completely in the end.

And where that doesn't work, the president's people will start, or boost, their own alternatives, and seek to route around you. Breitbart is just beginning.

5. You are going to have to get organized.

My sense is that American journalists aren't much for formal structures that reach across the profession and represent its interests.

The protection of the First Amendment, and your establishment credentials, have been enough, by and large. You don't have a press council, or a meaningful editors' body, or strong unions.

In the new world, Twitter journalism isn't going to be an adequate safeguard.

You need to band together around positive principles—independence, accountability, ethical standards, and the defense of your rights, which must be fought for both in the broad constitutional brushstrokes and the narrow detail of regulation and practice. Judging by the recent barrage of anti-Semitic and racist threats against journalists, you will also need to address both the climate of hate and specific concerns around safety.

Organizing journalists is a great deal worse than herding cats. We have egos that are at once giant and fragile. We like to own the story, all of it. We are rubbish at management. But some among you have these skills. Get it together to push them forward.

Also, find some allies outside of your usual circles. In South Africa, for example, our campaigns for freedom of information were vastly more credible when they were undertaken in partnership with organizations with their roots poor communities who could speak to the importance of transparency in ensuring access to clean water, safe streets, and health care.

I'm sorry to lecture. But I am worried. We all are. In the countries where I've spent my working life, the press still matters, but there is less of it, and the whole accountability ecosystem has become unbalanced. For all its real and urgent problems, US journalism is still the City on a Hill. The fading of its light will be disastrous not just for Americans, but for all of us.

CANADIAN JOURNALISTS WHO COVERED ROB FORD OFFER TIPS ON TRUMP

Bryan Borzykowski

(Toronto)

Originally published in *Columbia Journalism Review*
(November 25, 2016)

Americans would agree the United States has never seen a politician quite like Donald Trump. Constant falsehoods, attacks on newspapers, over-the-top insults directed at individual reporters—these are things many in the US media haven't had to deal with before. To Canadians, though, this type of media manipulation is all too familiar. For several years, former Toronto mayor Rob Ford treated journalists in much the same way.

The similarities between how these two politicians have approached the media is uncanny, says Daniel Dale, a *Toronto Star* journalist who covered Ford when he was in office and is now writing about Trump from Washington. Both politicians repeatedly and directly attacked particular media outlets, used the media to rile up their base, personally attacked journalists, and claim everything reported about them is false. "This is all very familiar to me," says Dale.

As stressful as it was to cover Ford, who passed away last March from cancer, the Canadian media now knows how to report on a post-truth, journalist-bashing politician and they have some ideas for their American counterparts struggling to keep up with Trump. The first piece of advice: Visuals speak louder than words.

GET VISUALS

No one knows that better than Robyn Doolittle, the now *Globe and Mail* reporter who was one of two *Toronto Star* journalists to see the infamous Ford crack-cocaine video. She was only allowed to watch the video on an iPhone in the backseat of a parked car—she couldn't take pictures or the video with her. While that seemed good enough at the time, when the story came out thousands of Torontonians, including Ford and other city councilors, said it was fake. "I was shocked that the half the city would think that the *Toronto Star* made up the story," she says.

About a year later, when she was now at the *Globe and Mail,* another drug dealer called saying he had a second video of Ford smoking crack. Once again, she could only watch the video on a mobile phone, but unlike with the first video, her paper agreed to pay ten thousand dollars for several screenshots. When the story came out the next day, Ford checked himself into rehab, something he had never done before. "I have a newfound appreciation for photos," she says. "In the days of Twitter, Instagram, and YouTube, people expect to see footage."

The power of visuals was on full display with the *Access Hollywood* tape where Trump boasted about his harassment of women. While papers reported on Trump's treatment of women before it aired, it was only after his comments were heard and seen that it became a national story.

STAND UP FOR YOURSELF

Journalists also have to start getting comfortable with defending themselves, says Dale. A year before the infamous crack video kicked Ford's disdain for the press into a higher gear, Dale went to see a small piece of property near Ford's home that the mayor had wanted to buy from the city. About twenty minutes after Dale arrived, Ford came out of his house, saw Dale nearby, and began yelling at him.

He then charged at him, only stopping when he saw that Dale was holding a cell phone, which had died a few minutes earlier.

That same night, Ford went on TV accusing Dale of trespassing on his property—this was an outright lie, as he was standing on city property—and then, months later, after the crack video had come out, he insinuated that Dale was a pedophile, saying he was standing in his backyard taking pictures of his kids. Of course, this also wasn't true.

While Dale didn't want to get into a fight with Ford, he was worried people might start questioning his credibility. He and his editors decided to hold a press conference where he would tell his side of the story. It was important for him to get on TV, he says, because "if Ford is giving people great video clips, even if he's lying, then I have to give video clips in response or else he would just dominate," he says. His editors also let him write a couple of columns. All of that, though, wasn't enough. After Ford accused Dale of taking pictures of his kids, he sued for defamation. It was only then that the mayor admitted his accusations weren't true.

US reporters may not sue their president for libel, but they do need to be as transparent as possible in their reporting, says Doolittle. She learned that people generally have no idea how the press goes about reporting a story, so the more reporters can demystify the process, the better. Doolittle made a point of being available for media interviews, which she admits is weird for reporters, but she felt it was necessary to explain to people how and why she wrote what she did. Her papers also started publishing behind-the-scenes stories to better explain to readers just how many checks and balances there are before a story goes to print.

HAVE SUPPORTIVE PUBLICATIONS

It's also critical for reporters to know their editors and their newspapers will be there to defend them, says Irene Gentle, managing editor at the *Toronto Star*. "Reporters have to believe they will be supported despite the attacks on them personally, despite the attacks on the integrity of the news organization and the news industry," she says. "The editor has to make that completely clear. The reporters have to know their job is to keep going."

At the same time, it's even more important that editors and reporters get the story right. Every allegation has to be checked out, every source vetted, and those sources shouldn't just be taking cheap shots. "The editor has to be with the reporters watching for this. It doesn't matter how dirty the fight against us is. We have to be clean in all ways," says Gentle. "With subjects such as Trump, and Ford in his time, the truth usually stands out pretty boldly in the end." Dale adds that reporters should try, as much as they can, to use on-the-record sources.

KEEP DOING YOUR JOB

There's no question reporting under these conditions is difficult, but Dale and Doolittle say they didn't do anything differently when it came to their reporting and never avoided publishing a story. Lisa Taylor, a journalism professor at Toronto's Ryerson University, says that journalists need to continue reporting what's in the public's interest, even if it seems as though the public isn't interested in what's being written. And while it was a challenge to be shut out of routine events, says Gentle—Ford didn't speak to the *Star* during his term—the paper always gave him the opportunity to comment before a story broke.

The hardest part for both Dale and Doolittle was not the accusations or attacks; it was that the public, and even friends, questioned their work. Dale recalls being at a wedding with acquaintances who asked him if he was sure that the crack video wasn't CGI. His friends still refer to the property incident as Fence-gate, even though he wasn't near Ford's fence. "When someone with that kind of megaphone sets a narrative, it's set," says Dale. Some people even still believe there was no crack video, even though the video ultimately did come to light, says Doolittle. "That's where it gets really frustrating or depressing," she says. "When you encounter people who just will not hear the truth."

At no time, though, did either reporter want to give up or move to another beat. As any good journalist does, they kept on digging, reporting, and writing. "There's an incredible amount of stress that goes with this, but it's still an amazing job," says Doolittle. "You just have to go out and do people proud."

A MESSAGE TO MY DOOMED COLLEAGUES IN THE AMERICAN MEDIA

Alexey Kovalev

(Russia)

Originally posted on Medium.com (January 12, 2017)

Congratulations, US media! You've just covered your first press conference of an authoritarian leader with a massive ego and a deep disdain for your trade and everything you hold dear. We in Russia have been doing it for twelve years now—with a short hiatus when our leader wasn't technically our leader—so quite a few things in Donald Trump's press conference rang a bell.

Vladimir Putin's annual pressers are supposed to be the media event of the year. They are normally held in late December, around Western Christmas time (we Orthodox Christians celebrate Christmas two weeks later and it's not a big deal, unlike New Year's Eve), which probably explains why Putin's pressers don't get much coverage outside of Russia, except in a relatively narrow niche of Russia-watchers. Putin's pressers are televised live across all Russian TV channels, attended by all kinds of media—federal news agencies, small local publications, and foreign reporters based in Moscow—and are supposed to overshadow every other event in Russia or abroad.

These things are carefully choreographed and typically last no less than four hours. Putin always comes off as an omniscient and benevolent leader tending to a flock of unruly but adoring children. Given that Putin is probably a role model for Trump, it's no surprise that Trump is apparently taking a page from Putin's playbook. I have some observations to share with my American colleagues. You're in this for at least another four years, and you'll be dealing with things Russian journalists have endured for almost two decades now. I'm talking about Putin here, but see if you can apply any of the below to your own leader.

WELCOME TO THE ERA OF BULLSHIT

Facts don't matter. You can't hurt this man with facts or reason. He'll always outmaneuver you. He'll always wriggle out of whatever carefully crafted verbal trap you lay for him. Whatever he says, you won't be able to challenge him. He always comes with a bag of meaningless factoids (Putin likes to drown questions he doesn't like in dull, unverifiable stats, figures, and percentages), platitudes, false moral equivalences, and straight, undiluted bullshit. He knows it's a one-way communication, not an interview. You can't follow up on your questions or challenge him. So he can throw whatever he wants at you in response, and you'll just have to swallow it. Some journalists will try to preempt this by asking two questions at once, against the protests of their colleagues also vying for attention, but that also won't work: He'll answer the one he thinks is easier, and ignore the other. Others will use this opportunity to go on a long, rambling statement vaguely disguised as a question, but that's also bad tactics. Nonquestions invite nonanswers. He'll mock you for your nervous stuttering and if you're raising a serious issue, respond with a vague, noncommittal statement. ("Mr. President, what about these horrible human rights abuses in our country?" "Thank you, miss. This is indeed a very serious issue. Everybody must respect the law. And by the way, don't human rights abuses happen in other countries as well? Next question please.")

But your colleagues are there to help you, right? After all, you're all in this together.

Wrong.

DON'T EXPECT ANY CAMARADERIE

These people are not your partners or brothers in arms. They are your rivals in a fiercely competitive, crashing market and right now the only currency in this market is whatever that man on the stage says. Whoever is lucky to ask a question and be the first to transmit the answer to the outside world wins. Don't expect any solidarity or support from them. If your question is stonewalled/mocked down/ignored, don't expect a rival publication to pick up the banner and follow up on your behalf. It's in this man's best interests to pit you against each other, fighting over artificial scarcities like room space, mic time, or, of course, his attention. It's getting especially absurd because some—increasingly many—reporters will now come with large, bright placards aimed at attracting the president's attention to names of their regions or specific issues.

Also, some people in the room aren't really there to ask questions.

EXPECT A LOT OF SYCOPHANCY AND
SOFTBALLS FROM YOUR "COLLEAGUES"

A mainstay of Putin's press conferences is, of course, softball questions. Which also happen to be Putin's favorites. Mr. President, is there love in your heart? Who will you be celebrating New Year's Eve with? What's your favorite food? "Questions" of this sort, sure to melt Putin's heart, typically come from women working for small regional publications. A subtype of this is also statements-as-questions, but from people who really love the man on the stage and will bob their head and look at the stage adoringly and say something to the tune of "Mr. President, do you agree that a lot of media are treating you unfairly?"

Another type of softball questions involves hyperlocal issues that a president isn't even supposed to be dealing with. Mr. President, our road is full of potholes and local authorities aren't doing anything about it. Mr. President, our tap is leaking. Mr. President, how about a chess club in our village. This is a real opportunity for him to shine. He will scold the local authorities and order to have a new road built. All of this, of course, has been choreographed well in advance.

Also, some of these people really love him and will meet his every answer with enthusiastic applause. There will be people from publications that exist for no other reason than heaping fawning praise on him and attacking his enemies. But there will also be one token critic who will be allowed to ask a "sharp" question, only to be drowned in a copious amount of bullshit, and the man on the stage will always be the winner ("See? I respect the media and free speech").

YOU'RE ALWAYS LOSING

This man owns you. He understands perfectly well that he is the news. You can't ignore him. You're always playing by his rules—which he can change at any time, without any notice. You can't—in Putin's case—campaign to vote him out of office. Your readership is dwindling because ad budgets are shrinking, while his ratings are soaring, and if you want to keep your publication afloat, you'll have to report on everything that man says as soon as he says it, without any analysis or fact-checking, because 1) his fans will not care if he lies to their faces; 2) while you're busy picking his lies apart, he'll spit out another mountain of bullshit and you'll be buried under it.

I could go on and on, but I think at this point you see where this is heading. See if any of this rings any bells if you covered Trump's presser or watched it online.

THE NEWS MEDIA HAS TO CHANGE OR IT'LL GET STEAMROLLED BY TRUMP*

Paul Waldman
(United States)

Originally published in *The American Prospect* (January 15, 2017)

Old habits and assumptions just won't cut it anymore.

For months, foolish people like myself suggested there was something problematic about the fact that Donald Trump had not held a press conference since July. How could he be held accountable without subjecting himself to interrogation by the press corps? Don't we need to at least see him confront some tough questions, in a situation where he can be called out when he lies and be forced to answer questions he'd rather avoid?

But Trump has a unique ability to make you question your assumptions. And after watching his first postelection press conference, one has to wonder whether there's much point in demanding that he do any more. In fact, it only highlighted the urgency for the nation's press corps to understand that covering this unusual president requires them to figure out a new way to do their jobs.

That press conference was no less of a Dumpster fire than Trump's entire presidential campaign. It was full of absurd claims—no, there are not "96 million really wanting a job and they can't get"—and full of Trump's usual petty vindictiveness, as he lashed out at the intelligence community, the Obama administration,

---

*Paul Waldman, "The News Media Has to Change or It'll Get Steamrolled by Trump," *American Prospect*, January 15, 2017, www.prospect.org.

Hillary Clinton, the Democratic Party, and of course the media. (About the only person who didn't come up for criticism was, naturally, Vladimir Putin.) He lobbed insults at news organizations (CNN is "fake news," BuzzFeed is "a failing pile of garbage"), had his staff whoop and cheer his answers, and brought out a pile of blank file folders apparently holding reams of blank paper, which he claimed were the papers he had to sign to disassociate from his businesses, which he's not actually disassociating himself from. At the end of it, one had to say: What was the point of that?

As we've seen again and again, Trump is willing to violate the norms that for years or decades have determined how government and politics operate. But that applies to the press, too—and reporters have to adapt. For instance, one of the assumptions underlying presidential press conferences is that the president feels at least some obligation to tell the truth, and some shame about being caught in a lie. If reporters do catch him lying, they'll press him on it, he'll squirm, and not only will the truth be revealed, but he'll be more likely to remain honest in the future so as to avoid a repeat of the experience.

But that doesn't apply to Trump. He lies so often and so obviously—sometimes for barely any discernible purpose—that calling him out on a lie to his face has no effect. He'll either repeat his lie or just move on to another one. In the context of a press conference, that gives him an advantage, at least insofar as his lie gets broadcast. Every Trump press conference is likely to turn into some version of this last one, where Trump acts in such a Trumpian way that no accountability is possible.

So what can the press do? They have to start questioning their own norms, and whether the way they've done business is tenable under this administration. That means casting off a few assumptions, including the following:

Direct questioning is the way to hold the president accountable. It's not that reporters should stop asking for interviews or boycott his press conferences, should he continue to have them. There have been interviews that have yielded important information and insights, sometimes for no other reason than they illustrate how pig-ignorant or hypocritical Trump is about some important topic. But they should keep their expectations low, and focus. Some collusion wouldn't hurt, either, as hard as it is to achieve in an intensely competitive business. For instance, they might decide together that they'll all ask about a single topic, in the hope that they might struggle their way through the hurricane of baloney Trump inevitably throws up. But neither the press conference nor the interview should be treated as the most important tool in the reporters' belt.

Access is critical. This has been a questionable assumption for a long time, but it's particularly important to discard it now. Yes, it makes reporters' jobs easier if they can get something like an inside scoop from sources as close as possible to the president. But those sources have always been more interested in using those contacts to push out the White House's spin, and with the most dishonest president in history, that spin is inevitably going to be even more misleading. In the campaign, the most valuable contributions were made by reporters like David Fahrenthold and Daniel Dale, who carved out an important niche and pursued it without relying on official sources. It can be a difficult thing to do if you're facing daily deadlines, but the chance that the most critical journalism in the Trump years will come from the person with the sources closest to Trump is approximately zero.

Critiquing the spectacle is important. The tendency to act like theater critics has long been a problem for political reporters, but it becomes even more problematic when they're covering a president who's primarily a celebrity entertainer. The point isn't that they shouldn't get underneath the show the White House is putting on, but that they need to do it in the right way. When Trump puts on photo ops trumpeting his heroic saving of a few hundred jobs, for instance, the question isn't what the visuals were like or whether it will "resonate" with some allegedly key voting bloc; it's how this one case fits in with the larger economic picture, and what kinds of results his policies are likely to produce.

Everything the president says—or tweets—is news. That's true to a degree, but we have to start with the assumption that what Trump says is highly likely to be false, or at the very least a childish distraction from more important things happening at the same time. That doesn't mean it shouldn't be discussed, but it should be discussed with the proper context. When Trump says that Representative John Lewis's Atlanta district is "in horrible shape and falling apart (not to mention crime infested)," the proper response is not "Ooh, snap! Trump's in another feud!" It's to point out that Lewis's district is in fact doing pretty well (it's the home of the Centers for Disease Control and Prevention, a bunch of colleges and universities including Georgia Tech, Emory, and Morehouse, and lots of thriving neighborhoods), and ask why the president-elect assumes that an African American congressman must represent a district out of some 1970s Charles Bronson urban-decay revenge thriller. In other words: If you must report the tweet, do it in a way that might actually teach your audience something important.

Unfortunately, following all these suggestions would make the already challenging job journalists have even harder. But as they should understand by now, the old ways of doing things just aren't going to work with this president—unless they want him to run roughshod over them and get away with anything.

JOURNALISM IN THE AGE OF TRUMP: LOSE THE SMUGNESS, KEEP THE MISSION

Margaret Sullivan

(United States)

Originally published in *The Washington Post* (November 29, 2016)

Journalists may thrive on news—by definition, the unexpected or novel—but they're terrible at getting out of their own comfortable ruts.

Consider, for example, the decade or so of abject denial about their threatened business model that followed the apocalyptic arrival of Craigslist, which removed the crucial revenue that came from classified advertising.

In short, we (yes, I include myself) don't handle change all that well.

And now we—the traditional, the legacy, the mainstream media—have to change.

Donald Trump has been a candidate and will be a president who requires vastly different coverage. If the 1970s brought, via Tom Wolfe, Joan Didion, and Norman Mailer, what was called "the New Journalism," I suggest we now need a New New Journalism.

Here are some ways journalism must be reinvented:

1. **Throw out the access-versus-accountability model.** Who gets the next coveted scoop? Often it has been that reporter who has most skillfully played the access game—the one who has curried just enough favor with the powerful newsmaker to be smiled

upon, without giving up basic credibility and integrity. That's access journalism.

Accountability journalism, by contrast, is often performed off to the side, by those who don't have to deal with the news provider on a regular basis. But with Trump, only those most willing to essentially, if unofficially, join the team themselves will get continued, dependable access. (Fox News's Sean Hannity, MSNBC's Joe Scarborough, and Bloomberg Politics's Mark Halperin come to mind.)

2. **Pick your spots.** Not everything Trump says or does deserves the same five-alarm level of outrage, or coverage. The president-elect's tweets criticizing the cast at the *Hamilton* musical are one thing. The proposed appointment of Jeff Sessions, with his history of racist behavior, as attorney general is quite another. (Rule of thumb: Tweets should get less attention. Actions should get more. Deep digging, even if not by one's own news organization, should get more still.)

Trump is, of course, a master of distraction and media manipulation. It's possible to resist being his chump, but it takes continued self-regulation.

3. **Realize the pointlessness of preaching to the choir.** As an inveterate student of reader comments, I can tell you that readers of liberal publications often are smart, articulate, and, for the most part, just as liberal as most of the columnists and editorial writers. It's swell, I suppose, that everyone is in agreement, but it accomplishes little.

If news organizations learned anything after the campaign, they should have learned that groupthink has a tendency to miss the point and journalistic myopia requires some extra-strength corrective lenses.

Do something different. Represent the interests of a broader, more ideologically diverse population. Figure out what they're thinking and feeling—and why.

4. **Develop a tougher skin.** Trump's use of the mainstream media as his favorite punching bag is only going to increase. That means

that his most fervent followers are going to hate traditional journalists, especially those from outlets in New York City and Washington.

It's no fun to be accused of rank stupidity or evildoing. It's especially hard to take when you believe in what you're writing or broadcasting and think it's important.

So what. It's just hyperbolic name-calling. Get over it. Do the work and don't expect to be loved.

5. **Call out craziness and falsehoods, knowing that you often won't be believed.** In the wacky new world of fake news, conspiracy theories, hoaxes—and social media's unthinking participation in spreading all of that—facts and truth get lost in the noise.

A responsible media needs to be especially careful not to unwittingly spread lies by amplifying them. Some early coverage of Trump's recent unwarranted, evidence-free blasts about the illegality of some of the popular vote fell into that trap.

It's depressing but a fact of life that a lot of people don't know the difference between fake news and conspiracy bilge and verified fact. Nor do they seem to care.

6. **Provide context.** This is another way of saying "Don't normalize," which is beginning to lose its meaning through repetition. For example, rather than calling Steve Bannon "alt-right" or, worse, "controversial," take some time to explain what he has done in making the Breitbart website a haven for white supremacists.

7. **Lose the smugness.** Keep the mission. Journalists need to stop thinking of themselves as so right and so much in the know. Quite obviously, they—we—often aren't. And, as David Eisenhower famously said, they aren't nearly as interesting as they think they are.

But the journalistic mission—holding the powerful accountable—remains crucially important. Maybe more than ever.

Is it possible for journalists to have a sense of humility about their work, even as they burn with purpose? That's a tough balance, bound to be elusive.

But it's a requirement of the New . . . New Journalism.

Part VI

Indivisible: A Practical Guide for Resisting the Trump Agenda

Editors' note: In December 2016, a group of former U.S. congressional staffers wrote and posted online a document titled Indivisible: A Practical Guide for Resisting the Trump Agenda. *Over the next month, the Guide was downloaded over 1,000,000 times and more than 4,500 local groups signed up to be part of the resistance effort outlined therein. The Guide is reprinted here in full, as updated January 27, 2017, by the original authors.*

NOTE TO IMMIGRANTS AND NONCITIZENS

The US Constitution ensures equal representation for all individuals living in the United States, regardless of income, race, ethnicity, gender, sexual orientation, age, or immigration status. Noncitizens, though they may lack the right to vote in federal elections, have the right to have their voices heard by their representatives in Congress.

This guide is intended to serve as a resource to all individuals who would like to more effectively participate in the democratic process. While we encourage noncitizens to participate to the extent that they are able, individuals should only take actions that they are comfortable taking, and they should consider their particular set of circumstances before engaging in any of these activities.

Individuals are under no obligation to provide any personally identifiable information to a member of Congress or their staff. Individuals may be asked for their name and zip code, but this is only to confirm that the person is a constituent, and providing this information is strictly voluntary. NO ONE is required to provide any additional information, such as address, Social Security number, or immigration status.

Updated by the Indivisible Team on January 27, 2017.

Indivisible: A Practical Guide for Resisting the Trump Agenda is licensed under the Creative Commons Attribution-NonCommercial-ShareAlike 4.0 International License. To view a copy of this license, visit http://creativecommons.org/licenses/by-nc-sa/4.0/.

A Partial List of Contributors to the Indivisible Guide:
Angel Padilla, Billy Fleming, Caroline Kavit, Emily Phelps, Ezra Levin, Gonzalo Martínez de Vedia, Indivar Dutta-Gupta, Jennay Ghowrwal, Jeremy Haile, Leah Greenberg, Mary Humphreys, Matt Traldi, Sara Clough, and Sarah Dohl.

INTRODUCTION

Donald Trump is the biggest popular-vote loser in history to ever call himself president-elect. In spite of the fact that he has no mandate, he will attempt to use his congressional majority to reshape America in his own racist, authoritarian, and corrupt image. If progressives are going to stop this, we must stand indivisibly opposed to Trump and the Members of Congress (MoCs) who would do his bidding. **Together, we have the power to resist—and we have the power to win.**

We know this because we've seen it before. The authors of this guide are former congressional staffers who witnessed the rise of the Tea Party. We saw these activists take on a popular president with a mandate for change and a supermajority in Congress. We saw them organize locally and convince their own MoCs to reject President Obama's agenda. Their ideas were wrong, cruel, and tinged with racism—and they won.

We believe that protecting our values, our neighbors, and ourselves will require mounting a similar resistance to the Trump agenda—but a resistance built on the values of inclusion, tolerance, and fairness. Trump is not popular. He does not have a mandate. He

---

WHO IS THIS DOCUMENT BY AND FOR?

We: Are former progressive congressional staffers who saw the Tea Party beat back President Obama's agenda.

We: See the enthusiasm to fight the Trump agenda and want to share insider info on how best to influence Congress to do that.

You: Want to do your part to beat back the Trump agenda, and understand that will require more than calls and petitions.

You: Should use this guide, share it, amend it, make it your own, and get to work.

does not have large congressional majorities. If a small minority in the Tea Party could stop President Obama, then we the majority can stop a petty tyrant named Trump.

To this end, the following chapters offer a step-by-step guide for individuals, groups, and organizations looking to replicate the Tea Party's success in getting Congress to listen to a small, vocal, dedicated group of constituents. The guide is intended to be equally useful for stiffening Democratic spines and weakening pro-Trump Republican resolve.

We believe that the next four years depend on Americans across the country standing indivisible against the Trump agenda. We believe that buying into false promises or accepting partial concessions will only further empower Trump to victimize us and our neighbors. We hope that this guide will provide those who share that belief with useful tools to make Congress listen.

SHORT SUMMARY

Here's the quick-and-dirty summary of this document. While this short summary provides top-level takeaways, the full document describes how to actually carry out these activities.

Chapter 1
How grassroots advocacy worked to stop President Obama. We examine lessons from the Tea Party's rise and recommend two key strategic components:

1. A local strategy targeting individual Members of Congress (MoCs).
2. A defensive approach purely focused on stopping Trump from implementing an agenda built on racism, authoritarianism, and corruption.

Chapter 2
How your MoC thinks—reelection, reelection, reelection—and how to use that to save democracy. MoCs want their constituents to think well of them, and they want good, local press. They hate surprises, wasted time, and most of all, bad press that makes them look weak, unlikable, and vulnerable. You will use these interests to make them listen and act.

Chapter 3
Identify or organize your local group. Is there an existing local group or network you can join? Or do you need to start your own? We suggest steps to help mobilize your fellow constituents locally and start organizing for action.

Chapter 4
Four local advocacy tactics that actually work. Most of you have three MoCs—two Senators and one Representative. Whether you like it or not, they are your voices in Washington. Your job is to make sure they are, in fact, speaking for you. We've identified four key opportunity areas that just a handful of local constituents can use to great effect. Always record encounters on video, prepare questions ahead of time, coordinate with your group, and report back to local media:

1. **Town halls.** MoCs regularly hold public in-district events to show that they are listening to constituents. Make them listen to you, and report out when they don't.
2. **Other local public events.** MoCs love cutting ribbons and kissing babies back home. Don't let them get photo ops without questions about racism, authoritarianism, and corruption.
3. **District office visits.** Every MoC has one or several district offices. Go there. Demand a meeting with the MoC. Report to the world if they refuse to listen.

4. **Coordinated calls.** Calls are a light lift, but they can have an impact. Organize your local group to barrage your MoCs at an opportune moment about and on a specific issue.

CHAPTER 1: HOW GRASSROOTS ADVOCACY WORKED TO STOP PRESIDENT OBAMA

If they succeed, or even half succeed, the Tea Party's most important legacy may be organizational, not political.
—Jonathan Rauch

Like us, you probably deeply disagree with the principles and positions of the Tea Party. But we can all learn from their success in influencing the national debate and the behavior of national policymakers. To their credit, they thought thoroughly about advocacy tactics, as the leaked "Town Hall Action Memo" demonstrates.

This chapter draws on both research and our own experiences as former congressional staffers to illustrate the strengths of the Tea Party movement and to provide lessons to leverage in the fight against Trump's racism, authoritarianism, and corruption.

The Tea Party's two key strategic choices
The Tea Party's success came down to two critical strategic elements:

1. They were locally focused. The Tea Party started as an organic movement built on small local groups of dedicated conservatives. Yes, they received some support/coordination from above, but fundamentally all the hubbub was caused by a relatively small number of conservatives working together.

- Groups started as disaffected conservatives talking to each other online. In response to the 2008 bank bailouts and President Obama's election, groups began forming to discuss their anger and what could be done. They eventually realized that the locally based discussion groups themselves could be a powerful tool.

- Groups were small, local, and dedicated. Tea Party groups could be fewer than 10 people, but they were highly localized, and they dedicated significant personal time and resources. Members communicated with each other regularly, tracked developments in Washington, and coordinated advocacy efforts together.
- Groups were relatively few in number. The Tea Party was not hundreds of thousands of people spending every waking hour focused on advocacy. Rather, the efforts were somewhat modest. Only 1 in 5 self-identified Tea Partiers contributed money or attended events. On any given day in 2009 or 2010, only 20 local events—meetings, trainings, town halls, etc.—were scheduled nationwide. In short, a relatively small number of groups were having a big impact on the national debate.

2. They were almost purely defensive. The Tea Party focused on saying NO to Members of Congress (MoCs) on their home turf. While the Tea Party activists were united by a core set of shared beliefs, they actively avoided developing their own policy agenda. Instead, they had an extraordinary clarity of purpose, united in opposition to President Obama. They didn't accept concessions and treated weak Republicans as traitors.

- Groups focused on defense, not policy development. In response to the 2008 bank bailouts and President Obama's election, groups began forming to discuss their anger and what could be done. They eventually realized that the locally based discussion groups themselves could be a powerful tool.
- Groups rejected concessions to Democrats and targeted weak Republicans. Tea Partiers viewed concessions to Democrats as betrayal. This limited their ability to negotiate, but they didn't

WHAT THE TEA PARTY ACCOMPLISHED

The Tea Party organized to end hope for progressive reform under President Obama.

Their members:

- Changed votes and defeated legislation
- Radically slowed federal policymaking
- Forced Republicans to reject compromise
- Shaped national debate over President Obama's agenda
- Paved the way for the Republican takeover in 2010 and Donald Trump today

These were real, tangible results by a group that represented only a small portion of Americans.

THE TEA PARTY'S IDEAS WERE WRONG

The Tea Party's ideas were wrong, and their behavior was often horrible. Their members:

- Ignored reality and made up their own facts
- Threatened anyone they considered an enemy
- Physically assaulted and spat on staff
- Shouted obscenities and burned people in effigy
- Targeted their hate not just at Congress, but also at fellow citizens (especially people of color)

We are better than this. We are the majority, and we don't need petty scare tactics to win.

care. Instead they focused on scaring congressional Democrats and keeping Republicans honest. As a result, few Republicans spoke against the Tea Party for fear of attracting blowback.
- Groups focused on local congressional representation. Tea Partiers primarily applied this defensive strategy by pressuring their own local MoCs. This meant demanding that their Representatives and Senators be their voice of opposition on

Capitol Hill. At a tactical level, the Tea Party had several repli-
cable practices, including:

- Showing up to the MoC's town hall meetings and demanding answers
- Showing up to the MoC's office and demanding a meeting
- Coordinating blanket calling of congressional offices at key
moments

Using These Lessons to Fight the Trump Agenda

For the next two years, Donald Trump and congressional Republicans will control the federal government. But they will depend on
just about every MoC to actually get laws passed. And those MoCs
care much more about getting reelected than they care about any
specific issue. By adopting a defensive strategy that pressures MoCs,
we can achieve the following goals:

- Stall the Trump agenda by forcing them to redirect energy
away from their priorities. Congressional offices have limited
time and limited people. A day that they spend worrying about
you is a day that they're not ending Medicare, privatizing public schools, or preparing a Muslim registry.
- Sap Representatives' will to support or drive reactionary
change. If you do this right, you will have an outsized impact. Every time your MoC signs on to a bill, takes a position,
or makes a statement, a little part of his or her mind will be
thinking: "How am I going to explain this to the angry constituents who keep showing up at my events and demanding
answers?"
- Reaffirm the illegitimacy of the Trump agenda. The hard
truth is that Trump, McConnell, and Ryan will have the votes
to cause some damage. But by objecting as loudly and pow-
erfully as possible, and by centering the voices of those who
are most affected by their agenda, you can ensure that people

---

SHOULDN'T WE PUT FORWARD AN ALTERNATE, POSITIVE AGENDA?

A defensive strategy does not mean dropping your own policy priorities or staying silent on an alternate vision for our country over the next four years. What it means is that, when you're trying to influence your MoC, you will have the most leverage when you are focused on the current legislative priority.

You may not like the idea of being purely defensive; we certainly don't. As progressives, our natural inclination is to talk about the things we're for—a clean climate, economic justice, health care for all, racial equality, gender and sexual equality, and peace and human rights. These are the things that move us. But the hard truth of the next four years is that we're not going to set the agenda; Trump and congressional Republicans will, and we'll have to respond. The best way to stand up for the progressive values and policies we cherish is to stand together, indivisible—to treat an attack on one as an attack on all.

---

understand exactly how bad these laws are from the very start—priming the ground for the 2018 midterms and their repeal when Democrats retake power

CHAPTER 2: HOW YOUR MEMBER OF CONGRESS THINKS, AND HOW TO USE THAT TO SAVE DEMOCRACY

There go the people. I must follow them, for I am their leader.
—Alexandre Ledru-Rollin

This chapter explains how congressional offices and the people within them work, and what that means for your advocacy strategy.

It's All About Reelection, Reelection, Reelection

To influence your own Member of Congress (MoC), you have to understand one thing: every House member runs for office every two years and every Senator runs for election every six years. Functionally speaking, MoCs are always either running for office or getting ready for their next election—a fact that shapes everything they do.

To be clear, this does not mean that your MoC is cynical and unprincipled. The vast majority of people in Congress believe in their ideals and care deeply about representing their constituents and having a positive impact. But they also know that if they want to make change, they need to stay in office.

This constant reelection pressure means that MoCs are enormously sensitive to their image in the district or state, and they will work very hard to avoid signs of public dissent or disapproval. What every MoC wants—regardless of party—is for his or her constituents to agree with the following narrative:

> *"My MoC cares about me, shares my values, and is working hard for me."*
>
> —What every MoC wants their constituents to think

HELP, MY MEMBER OF CONGRESS IS IN A SAFE DISTRICT

If your actions threaten this narrative, then you will unnerve your MoC and change their decision-making process. If your MoC is in a heavily Democratic or Republican district, you may assume that they have a safe seat and there's nothing you can do to influence them. This is not true! The reality is that no MoC ever considers themselves to be safe from all threats. MoCs who have nothing to fear from a general election still worry about primary challenges.

More broadly, no one stays an MoC without being borderline compulsive about protecting their image. Even the safest MoC will be deeply alarmed by signs of organized opposition, because these actions create the impression that they're not connected to their district and not listening to their constituents.

HELP, MY MOCS ARE ACTUALLY PRETTY GOOD!

Congratulations! Your Senators and Representative are doing what they should to fight racism, authoritarianism, and corruption. They're making the right public statements, co-sponsoring the right bills, and voting the right way. So how does this change your strategy? Two key things to keep in mind:

Do NOT switch to targeting other MoCs who don't represent you. They don't represent you, and they don't care what you have to say. Stick with your own local MoCs.

DO use this guide to engage with your MoCs locally. Instead of pressuring them to do the right thing, praise them for doing the right thing. This is important because it will help ensure that they continue to do the right thing. Congressional staff are rarely contacted when the MoC does something good—your efforts locally will provide highly valuable positive reinforcement.

What Does a MoC's Office Do, and Why?

A MoC's office is composed of roughly 15–25 staff for House offices and 60–70 for Senate offices, spread across a D.C. office and one or several district offices. MoC offices perform the following functions:

- **Provide constituent services.** Staff connect with both individual constituents and local organizations, serving as a link to and an advocate within the federal government on issues such as visas, grant applications, and public benefits.
- **Communicate with constituents directly.** Staff take calls, track constituent messages, and write letters to stay in touch with constituents' priorities, follow up on specific policy issues that constituents have expressed concern about, and reinforce the message that they are listening.
- **Meet with constituents.** MoCs and staff meet with constituents to learn about local priorities and build connections.

- **Seek and create positive press.** Staff try to shape press coverage and public information to create a favorable image for the MoC.
- **Host and attend events in district.** Representatives host and attend events in the district to connect with constituents, understand their priorities, and get good local press.
- **Actual legislating.** MoCs and staff decide their policy positions, develop and sponsor bills, and take votes based on a combination of their own beliefs, pressure from leadership/lobbyists, and pressure from their constituents.

What Your MoC Cares About

When it comes to constituent interactions, MoCs care about things that make them look good, responsive, and hardworking to the people of their district. In practice, that means that they care about some things very much, and other things very little:

YOUR MOC CARES A LOT ABOUT	YOUR MOC DOESN'T CARE MUCH ABOUT
Verified constituents from the district (or state for Senators)	People from outside the district (or state for Senators)
Advocacy that requires effort— the more effort, the more they care: calls, personal emails, and especially showing up in person in the district	Form letters, a tweet, or a Facebook comment (unless they generate widespread attention)
Local press and editorials, maybe national press	Wonky D.C.-based news (depends on the MoC)
An interest group's endorsement	Your thoughtful analysis of the proposed bill
Groups of constituents, locally famous individuals, or big individual campaign contributors	A single constituent

YOUR MOC CARES A LOT ABOUT	YOUR MOC DOESN'T CARE MUCH ABOUT
Concrete asks that entail a verifiable action—vote for a bill, make a public statement, etc.	General ideas about the world
A single ask in your communication—letter, email, phone call, office visit, etc	A laundry list of all the issues you're concerned about

What Your MoC Is Thinking:
Good Outcome vs. Bad Outcome

To make this a bit more concrete and show where advocacy comes in, below are some examples of actions that a MoC might take, what they're hoping to see happen as a result, and what they really don't want to see happen. Some MoCs will go to great lengths to avoid bad outcomes—even as far as changing their positions or public statements.

EXAMPLE ACTION	DESIRED OUTCOME	BAD OUTCOME
Letter to Constituent	Constituent feels happy that their concerns were answered.	Constituent posts letter on social media saying it didn't answer their questions or neglected their questions for weeks/months, calls Congressman Bob unresponsive and untrustworthy.
In-district Event	Local newspaper reports that Congresswoman Sara appeared at opening of new bridge, for which she helped secure funding.	Local newspaper reports that protesters barraged Congresswoman Sara with questions about corruption in the infrastructure bill.

(*continued on next page*)

EXAMPLE ACTION	DESIRED OUTCOME	BAD OUTCOME
Town Hall / Listening Session	Local newspaper reports that Congressman Bob hosted a town hall and discussed his work to balance the budget.	Local newspaper reports that angry constituents strongly objected to Congressman Bob's support for privatizing Medicare.
Policy Position	Congresswoman Sara votes on a bill and releases a press statement hailing it as a step forward.	Congresswoman Sara's phones are deluged with calls objecting to the bill. A group of constituents stage an event outside her district office and invite press to hear them talk about how the bill will personally hurt their families.

CHAPTER 3: ORGANIZE A LOCAL GROUP TO FIGHT FOR YOUR CONGRESSIONAL DISTRICT

We need in every bay and community a group of angelic troublemakers.

—Bayard Rustin

The Tea Party formed organically as conservatives upset after the 2008 election came together in local discussion groups. We believe the same thing is happening now across the country as progressives—in person, in already existing networks, and on Facebook—come together to move forward. The big question for these groups is: what's next?

If you're reading this, you're probably already part of a local network of people who want to stop the Trump agenda—even if it's just your friends or a group on Facebook. This chapter is about how to take that energy to the next level and start fighting locally to take the country back.

Should I Form a Group?

There's no need to reinvent the wheel—if an activist group or network is already attempting to do congressional advocacy along these lines, just join them. Depending on your Representative's district, it may make sense to have more than one group. This congressional map tool (https://www.govtrack.us/congress/members/map) shows the boundaries for your district.

If you look around and can't find a group working specifically on local action focused on your Members of Congress (MoCs) in your area, just start doing it! It's not rocket science. You really just need two things:

- Ten or so people (but even fewer is a fine start!) who are geographically nearby—ideally in the same congressional district.

DIVERSITY IN YOUR GROUP & REACHING OUT

Trump's agenda explicitly targets immigrants, Muslims, people of color, LGBTQ people, the poor and working class, and women. It is critical that our resistance reflect and center the voices of those who are most directly threatened by the Trump agenda. If you are forming a group, we urge you to make a conscious effort to pursue diversity and solidarity at every stage in the process. Being inclusive and diverse might include recruiting members who can bridge language gaps, and finding ways to accommodate participation when people can't attend due to work schedules, health issues, or childcare needs.

In addition, where there are local groups already organizing around the rights of those most threatened by the Trump agenda, we urge you to reach out to partner with them, amplify their voices, and defer to their leadership.

- A commitment from those people to devote a couple of hours per month to fighting the racism, authoritarianism, and corruption pushed by Trump.

How to Form a Group

If you do want to form a group, here are our recommendations on how to go about it:

1. **Decide you're going to start a local group** dedicated to making your MoCs aware of their constituents' opposition to the Trump agenda. This might be a subgroup of an existing activist group, or it might be a new effort—it really depends on your circumstances. Start where people are: if you're in a group with a lot of people who want to do this kind of thing, then start there; if you're not, you'll need to find them somewhere else. The most important thing is that this is a LOCAL group. Your band of heroes is focused on applying local pressure, which means you all need to be local.
2. **Identify a few additional cofounders** who are interested in participating and recruiting others. Ideally, these are people who have different social networks from you so that you can maximize your reach. Make an effort to ensure that leadership of the group reflects the diversity of opposition to Trump.
3. **Email your contacts and post a message on your Facebook page**, on any local Facebook groups that you're a member of, and/or other social media channels you use regularly. Say that you're starting a group for constituents of Congresswoman Sara, dedicated to stopping the Trump agenda, and ask people to email you to sign up.
4. **Invite everyone who has expressed interest to an in-person kickoff meeting.** Use this meeting to agree on a name, principles for your group, roles for leadership, a way of communicating, and a strategy for your MoC. Rule of thumb: 50%

HOW DO I RECRUIT PEOPLE TO TAKE ACTION?

Most people are moved to take action through individual conversations. Here are some tips for having successful conversations to inspire people to take action with your group.

1. **Get the story.** What issues does the other person care about? How would the reactionary Republican agenda affect them, their communities, and their values?
2. **Imagine what's possible.** How can your group change your community's relationship with your MoC? How can your group, and others like it, protect our values?
3. **Commitment and ownership.** Ask a clear yes-or-no question: will you work with me to hold our representatives accountable? Then, get to specifics. Who else can they talk to about joining the group? What work needs to be done—planning a meeting, researching a MoC—that they can take on? When will you follow up?

Ask open-ended questions! People are more likely to take action when they articulate what they care about and can connect it to the action they are going to take. A good rule of thumb is to talk 30% of the time or less and listen at least 70% of the time.

---

of the people who have said they are definitely coming will show up to your meeting. Aim high! Get people to commit to come—they'll want to because saving democracy is fun.

- **Manage the meeting:** Keep people focused on the ultimate core strategy: applying pressure to your MoC to stop Trump. Other attendees may have other ideas—or may be coming to share their concerns about Trump—and it's important to affirm their concerns and feelings. But it's also important to redirect that energy and make sure that the conversation stays focused on developing a group and a plan of action dedicated to this strategy.

- **Decide on a name:** Good names include the geographic area of your group, so that it's clear that you're rooted in the community—e.g., "Springfield Indivisible Against Hate." You are 100% welcome to pick up and run with the Indivisible name if you want, but we won't be hurt if you don't.
- **Agree on principles:** This is your chance to say what your group stands for. We recommend two guiding principles:

  - Donald Trump's agenda will take America backwards, and it must be stopped.
  - To work together to achieve this goal, we must model the values of inclusion, tolerance, and fairness.

  As discussed in the second chapter, we strongly recommend focusing on defense against the Trump agenda rather than developing an entire alternative policy agenda. Defining a proactive agenda is time-intensive, divisive, and, quite frankly, a distraction, since there is zero chance that we as progressives will get to put our agenda into action at the federal level in the next four years.
- **Volunteer for roles:** Figure out how to divide roles and responsibilities among your group. This can look very different depending on who's in the room, but at a minimum, you probably want 1–2 people in charge of overall group coordination, a designated media/social media contact, and 1–2 people in charge of tracking the congressional office's schedule and events. In addition to these administrative roles, ask attendees how they want to contribute to advocacy efforts: attend events, record events, ask questions, make calls, host meetings, engage on social media, write op-eds for local papers, etc.
- **Adopt means of communication:** You need a way of reaching everyone in your group in order to coordinate actions. This can be a Facebook group, a Google group, a Slack

team—whatever people are most comfortable with. It may be wise to consider secure or encrypted platforms such as Signal and WhatsApp.

5. **Expand!** Enlist your members to recruit across their networks. Ask every member to send out the same outreach emails/ posts that you did.

- Recruit people for your email list—100 or 200 isn't unreasonable.
- We strongly recommend making a conscious effort to diversify your group and particularly to center around and defer to communities of people who are most directly affected by the Trump administration's racism, xenophobia, transphobia, homophobia, and antipathy toward the poor. This could include both reaching out through your own networks and forming relationships with community groups that are already working on protecting the rights of marginalized groups.

ALREADY HAVE A GROUP?

Sign up at www.indivisibleguide.com. We're creating a public directory of groups to help you make connections on your home turf. We'll also be sending special updates to group leaders to help build local congressional action plans.

Your group may be pursuing the Indivisible strategy as your main goal or as part of a broader mission. Whatever works!

CHAPTER 4: FOUR LOCAL ADVOCACY
TACTICS THAT ACTUALLY WORK

Every moment is an organizing opportunity, every person a potential activist, every minute a chance to change the world.

—Dolores Huerta

This chapter describes the nuts and bolts of implementing four advocacy tactics to put pressure on your three Members of Congress (MoCs)—your Representative and two Senators. Before we get there, though, there are a few things all local groups should do:

Begin with these five steps to gather intel. Before anything else, take the following five steps to arm yourself with information necessary for all future advocacy activities.

1. Find your three MoCs, their official websites, and their office contact info at www.callmycongress.com.
2. Sign up on your MoCs' websites to receive regular email updates, invites to local events, and propaganda to understand what they're saying. Every MoC has an e-newsletter.
3. Find out where your MoCs stand on the issues of the day—appointment of white supremacists, tax cuts for the rich, etc. Review their voting history at VoteSmart.org. Research their biggest campaign contributors at OpenSecrets.org.
4. Set up a Google News Alert (http://www.google.com/alerts)—for example for "Rep. Bob Smith"—to receive an email whenever your MoCs are in the news.
5. Research on Google News (https://news.google.com/news) what local reporters have written about your MoCs. Find and follow those reporters on Twitter, and build relationships. Before you attend or plan an event, reach out and explain why your group is protesting, and provide them with background materials and a quote. Journalists on deadline—even those

---

NOTE ON SAFETY AND PRIVILEGE

We do not yet know how Trump supporters will respond to organized shows of opposition, but we have seen enough to be very concerned that minorities will be targeted or singled out. Plan your actions to ensure that no one is asked to take on a role that they are not comfortable with—especially those roles that call for semi-confrontational behavior—and be mindful of the fact that not everyone is facing an equal level of threat. Members of your group who enjoy more privilege should think carefully about how they can ensure that they are using their privilege to support other members of the group. If you are concerned about potential law enforcement intimidation, consider downloading your state's version of the ACLU Mobile Justice app to ensure that any intimidating behavior is captured on film. Please familiarize yourself with your state and local laws that govern recording, along with any applicable Senate or House rules, prior to recording. These laws and rules vary substantially from jurisdiction to jurisdiction.

---

who might not agree with you—appreciate when you provide easy material for a story.

Opportunity 1
Town Halls/Listening Sessions
MoCs regularly hold local "town halls" or public listening sessions throughout their districts or state. Tea Partiers used these events to great effect—both to directly pressure their MoCs and to attract media to their cause.

Preparation
1. **Find out when your MoC's next public town hall event is.** Sometimes these are announced well in advance, and sometimes, although they are technically "public," only select constituents are notified about them shortly before the event. If you can't find announcements online, call your MoC directly

to find out. When you call, be friendly and say to the staffer, "Hi, I'm a constituent, and I'd like to know when his/her next town hall forum will be." If they don't know, ask to be added to the email list so that you get notified when they do.

2. **Send out a notice of the town hall to your group, and get commitments from members to attend.** Distribute to all of them whatever information you have on your MoC's voting record, as well as the prepared questions.

3. **Prepare several questions ahead of time for your group to ask.** Your questions should be sharp and fact-based, ideally including information on the MoC's record, votes they've taken, or statements they've made. Thematically, questions should focus on a limited number of issues to maximize impact. Prepare 5–10 of these questions and hand them out to your group ahead of the meeting. Example question:

"I and many district families in Springfield rely on Medicare. I don't think we should be rationing health care for seniors, and the plan to privatize Medicare will create serious financial hardship for seniors who can't afford it. You haven't gone on the record opposing this. Will you commit here and now to vote no on Bill X to cut Medicare?"

SHOULD I BRING A SIGN?

Signs can be useful for reinforcing the sense of broad agreement with your message. However, if you're holding an oppositional sign, staffers will almost certainly not give you or the people with you the chance to get the mic or ask a question. If you have enough people to both ask questions and hold signs, though, then go for it!

At the Town Hall

1. **Get there early, meet up, and get organized.** Meet outside or in the parking lot for a quick huddle before the event. Distribute the handout of questions, and encourage members to ask the questions on the sheet or something similar.

2. **Get seated and spread out.** Head into the venue a bit early to grab seats at the front half of the room, but do not all sit together. Sit by yourself or in groups of two, and spread out throughout the room. This will help reinforce the impression of broad consensus.

3. **Make your voices heard by asking good questions.** When the MoC opens the floor for questions, everyone in the group should put their hands up and keep them there. Look friendly or neutral so that staffers will call on you. When you're asking a question, remember the following guidelines:

   - **Stick with the prepared list of questions.** Don't be afraid to read it straight from the printout if you need to.
   - **Be polite but persistent, and demand real answers.** MoCs are very good at deflecting or dodging questions they don't want to answer. If the MoC dodges, ask a follow-up question. If they aren't giving you real answers, then call them out for it. Other group members around the room should amplify by either booing the MoC or applauding you.
   - **Don't give up the mic until you're satisfied with the answer.** If you've asked a hostile question, a staffer will often try to limit your ability to follow up by taking the microphone back immediately after you finish speaking. They can't do that if you keep a firm hold on the mic. No staffer in their right mind wants to look like they're physically intimidating a constituent, so they will back off. If they object, then say politely but loudly: "I'm not finished. The MoC is dodging my question. Why are you trying to stop me from following up?"

- **Keep the pressure on.** After one member of the group finishes, everyone should raise their hands again. The next member of the group to be called on should move down the list of questions and ask the next one.

4. **Support the group and reinforce the message.** After one member of your group asks a question, everyone should applaud to show that the feeling is shared throughout the audience. Whenever someone from your group gets the mic, they should note that they're building on the previous questions—amplifying the fact that you're part of a broad group.

5. **Record everything!** Assign someone in the group to use their smartphone or video camera to record other advocates asking questions and the MoC's response. While written transcripts are nice, unfavorable exchanges caught on video can be devastating for MoCs. These clips can be shared through social media and picked up by local and national media. Please familiarize yourself with your state and local laws that govern recording, along with any applicable Senate or House rules, prior to recording. These laws and rules vary substantially from jurisdiction to jurisdiction.

After the Town Hall

1. **Reach out to media, during and after the town hall.** If there's media at the town hall, the people who asked questions should approach them afterward and offer to speak about their concerns. When the event is over, you should engage local reporters on Twitter or by email and offer to provide an in-person account of what happened, as well as the video footage you collected. Example Twitter outreach:

   @reporter I was at Rep. Smith's town hall in Springfield today. Large group asked about Medicare privatization. I have video & happy to chat.

Note: It's important to make this a public tweet by including the period before the journalist's Twitter handle. Making this public will make the journalist more likely to respond to ensure they get the intel first.

Ensure that the members of your group who are directly affected by specific threats are the ones whose voices are elevated when you reach out to media.

2. **Share everything.** Post pictures, video, your own thoughts about the event, etc., to social media afterward. Tag the MoC's office and encourage others to share widely.

Opportunity 2
Other Local Public Events
In addition to town halls, MoCs regularly attend public events for other purposes—parades, infrastructure groundbreakings, etc. Like town halls, these are opportunities to get face time with the MoCs and make sure they're hearing about your concerns, while simultaneously changing the news story that gets written.

Similar to town halls, but with some tweaks. To take advantage of this opportunity, you can follow most of the guidelines above for town halls (filming, etc.). However, because these events are not designed for constituent input, you will need to think creatively about how to make sure your presence and message come through loud and clear.

Tactics for these events may be similar to more traditional protests, where you're trying to shift attention from the scheduled event to your own message.

1. **Optimize visibility.** Unlike in town halls, you want your presence as a group to be recognizable and attention-getting at this event. It may make sense to stick together as a group, wear relatively similar clothing/message shirts, and carry signs in order to be sure that your presence is noticeable.

2. **Be prepared to interrupt and insist on your right to be heard.** Since you won't get the mic at an event like this, you have to attract attention to yourself and your message. Agree beforehand with your group on a simple message focused on a current or upcoming issue. Coordinate with each other to chant this message during any public remarks that your MoC makes. This can be difficult and a bit uncomfortable. But it sends a powerful message to your MoC that they won't be able to get press for other events until they address your concerns.

3. **Identify, and try to speak with, reporters on the scene.** Be polite and friendly, and stick to your message. For example, "We're here to remind Congresswoman Sara that her constituents are opposed to Medicare cuts." You may want to research in advance which local reporters cover MoCs or relevant beats, so that you know who to look for.

4. **Hold organizational hosts accountable.** Often these events will be hosted by local businesses or nonpartisan organizations— groups that don't want controversy or to alienate the community. Reach out to them directly to express your concern that they are giving a platform to pro-Trump authoritarianism, racism, and corruption. If they persist, use social media to express your disappointment. This will reduce the likelihood that these organizations will host the Trump-friendly MoC in the future. MoCs depend on invitations like these to build ties and raise their visibility—so this matters to them.

Opportunity 3
District Office Visits
Every MoC has at least one district office, and many MoCs have several spread through their district or state. These are public offices, open for anybody to visit—you don't need an appointment. You can take advantage of this to stage an impromptu town hall meeting by showing up with a small group. It is much harder for district or D.C.

staff to turn away a group than a single constituent, even without an appointment.

1. **Find out where your MoCs' local offices are.** The official Web page for your MoC will list the address of every local office. You can find those Web pages easily through a simple Google search. In most cases, the URL for a House member will be www.[lastname].house.gov, and the URL for Senate offices is www.[lastname].senate.gov.
2. **Plan a trip when the MoC is there.** Most MoC district offices are open only during regular business hours, 9 a.m.–5 p.m. While MoCs spend a fair amount of time in Washington, they are often "in district" on Mondays and Fridays, and there are weeks designated for MoCs to work in district. The MoC is most likely to be at the "main" office—the office in the largest city in the district, and where the MoC's district director works. Ideally, plan a time when you and several other people can show up together.
3. **Prepare several questions ahead of time.** As with the town halls, you should prepare a list of questions ahead of time.
4. **Politely, but firmly, ask to meet with the MoC directly.** Staff will ask you to leave or at best "offer to take down your concerns." Don't settle for that. You want to speak with the MoC directly. If they are not in, ask when they will next be in. If the staffer doesn't know, tell them you will wait until they find out. Sit politely in the lobby. Note: on any given weekend, the MoC may or may not actually come to that district office.
5. **Note that office sit-ins can backfire,** so be very thoughtful about the optics of your visit. This tactic works best when you are protesting an issue that directly affects you and/or members of your group (e.g., seniors and caregivers on Medicare cuts, or Muslims and allies protesting a Muslim registry). Being polite and respectful throughout is critical.
6. **Meet with the staffer.** Even if you are able to get a one-off

meeting with the MoC, you are most often going to be meeting with their staff. In district, the best person to meet with is the district director, or the head of the local district office you're visiting. There are real advantages to building a relationship with these staff. In some cases, they may be more open to progressive ideas than the MoC, and having a good meeting with/building a relationship with a supportive staff member can be a good way to move your issue up the chain of command. Follow these steps for a good staff meeting:

- Have a specific "ask"—e.g., vote against X, cosponsor Y, publicly state Z, etc.
- Leave staff with a **brief** write-up of your issue, with your ask clearly stated.
- Share a personal story of how you or someone in your group is personally impacted by the specific issue (health care, immigration, Medicare, etc.).
- Be polite—yelling at the underpaid, overworked staffer won't help your cause.
- Be persistent—get their business card and call/email them regularly; ask if the MoC has taken action on the issue.

7. **Advertise what you're doing.** Communicate on social media, and tell the local reporters you follow what is happening. Take and send pictures and videos with your group: "At Congresswoman Sara's office with 10 other constituents to talk to her about privatizing Medicare. She refuses to meet with us and staff won't tell us when she will come out. We're waiting."

Opportunity 1
Coordinated Calls
Mass office calling is a light lift, but it can actually have an impact. Tea Partiers regularly flooded congressional offices with calls at opportune moments, and MoCs noticed.

1. **Find the phone numbers for your MoCs.** You can find your local MoCs and their office phone numbers at www.callmy congress.com.

2. **Prepare a single question per call.** For in-person events, you want to prepare a host of questions, but for calls, keep it simple. You and your group should all agree to call in on one specific issue that day. The question should be about a live issue—e.g., a vote that is coming up, a chance to take a stand, or some other time-sensitive opportunity. The next day or week, pick another issue, and call again on that.

3. **Find out who you're talking to.** In general, the staffer who answers the phone will be an intern, a staff assistant, or some other very junior staffer in the MoC's office. But you want to talk to the legislative staffer who covers the issue you're calling about. There are two ways to do this:

   - Ask to speak to the staffer who handles the issue (immigration, health care, etc.). Junior staff are usually directed to not tell you who this is, and instead just take down your comment.
   - On a different day, call and ask whoever answers the phone, "Hi, can you confirm the name of the staffer who covers [immigration/health care/etc.]?" Staff will generally tell you the name. Say "Thanks!" and hang up. Ask for the staffer by name when you call back next time.

4. **If you're directed to voicemail, follow up with email.** Then follow up again. Getting more-senior legislative staff on the phone is tough. The junior staffer will probably just tell you "I checked, and she's not at her desk right now, but would you like to leave a voicemail?" Go ahead and leave a voicemail, but don't expect a call back. Instead, after you leave that voicemail, follow up with an email to the staffer. If they still don't

respond, follow up again. If they still don't respond, let the world know that the MoC's office is dodging you.

Congressional emails are standardized, so even if the MoC's office won't divulge that information, you can probably guess it if you have the staffer's first and last name.

- **Senate email addresses:** For the Senate, the formula is: StafferFirstName_StafferLastName@MoCLastName.senate.gov. For example, if Jane Doe works for Senator Roberts, her email address is likely "Jane_Doe@roberts.senate.gov"
- **House email addresses:** For the House, the formula is simpler: StafferFirstName.StafferLastName@mail.house.gov. For example, if Jane Doe works in the House, her email address is likely "Jane.Doe@mail.house.gov"

5. **Keep a record of the conversation.** Take detailed notes on everything the staffer tells you. Direct quotes are great, and anything they tell you is public information that can be shared widely. Compare notes with the rest of your group, and identify any conflicts in what they're telling constituents.

6. **Report back to media and your group.** Report back to both your media contacts and your group what the staffer said when you called.

SAMPLE CALL DIALOGUE

STAFFER: Congresswoman Sara's office, how can I help you?

CALLER: Hi there, I'm a constituent of Congresswoman Sara's. Can I please speak with the staffer who handles presidential appointments issues?

STAFFER: I'm happy to take down any comments you may have. Can I ask for your name and address to verify you're in the Congresswoman's district?

CALLER: Sure thing. [Gives name/address]. Can I ask who I'm speaking with?

STAFFER: Yes, this is Jeremy Smith.

CALLER: Thanks, Jeremy! I'm calling to ask what the Congresswoman is doing about the appointment of Steve Bannon to serve in the White House. Bannon is reported as saying he didn't want his children to go to a school with Jews. And he ran a website that promoted white nationalist views. I'm honestly scared that a known racist and anti-Semite will be working just feet from the Oval Office. Can you tell me what Congresswoman Sara is going to do about it?

STAFFER: Well I really appreciate you calling and sharing your thoughts! I of course can't speak for the Congresswoman because I'm just a staff assistant, but I can tell you that I'll pass your concerns on to her.

CALLER: I appreciate that, Jeremy, but I don't want you to just pass my concerns on. I would like to know what the Congresswoman is doing to stop this.

[If they stick with the "I'm just a staffer" line, ask them when a more senior staffer will get back to you with an answer to your question.]

STAFFER: I'm afraid we don't take positions on personnel appointments.

CALLER: Why not?

STAFFER: Personnel appointments are the President's responsibility. We have no control over them.

CALLER: But Congresswoman Sara has the ability to speak out and say that this is unacceptable. Other members of Congress have done so. Why isn't Congresswoman Sara doing that?

STAFFER: As I said, this is the President's responsibility. It's not our business to have a position on who he chooses for his staff.

(continued on next page)

> **CALLER:** It is everyone's business if a man who promoted white supremacy is serving as an adviser to the President. The Congresswoman is my elected representative, and I expect her to speak out on this.
>
> **STAFFER:** I'll pass that on.
>
> **CALLER:** I find it unacceptable that the Congresswoman refuses to take a position. I'll be notifying my friends, family, and local newspaper that our Congresswoman doesn't think it's her job to represent us or actually respond to her constituents' concerns.

Change will not come if we wait for some other person or some other time. We are the ones we've been waiting for. We are the change that we seek.

—President Barack Obama

We wrote this guide because we believe that the coming years will see an unprecedented movement of Americans rising up across the country to protect our values, our neighbors, and ourselves. Our goal is to provide practical understanding of how your Members of Congress (MoCs) think, and how you can demonstrate to them the depth and power of the opposition to Donald Trump and to Republican congressional overreach. This is not a panacea, and it is not intended to stand alone. We strongly urge you to marry the strategy in this guide with a broader commitment to creating a more just society, building local power, and addressing systemic injustice and racism.

Finally, this guide is intended as a work in progress, one that we hope to continue updating as the resistance to the Trump agenda takes shape. We are happy to offer support to anybody interested in building upon the tactics outlined in this guide, and we hope that if you find it useful or put any of the tactics described above into action, you will let us know how it goes. Feel free to ping some of us on

Twitter with questions, edits, recommendations, feedback/stories about what is helpful here, etc.: @IndivisibleTeam, @ezralevin, @angelrafpadilla, @texpat, @Leahgreenb. Or email Indivisible AgainstTrump@gmail.com.

Good luck—we will win.

CONTRIBUTOR BIOGRAPHIES

Rana Allam is former chief editor of *Daily News Egypt,* with a journalism career dating back to 1995. She is currently an adviser and editor to the International Civil Action Network and the Women Alliance for Security Leadership organizations.

Anne Applebaum writes a weekly foreign affairs column for *The Washington Post* and is a Pulitzer Prize–winning historian. She is a professor of practice at the London School of Economics.

Peter Apps is a Reuters global affairs columnist, writing on international affairs, globalization, conflict, and other issues. He is founder and executive director of the Project for Study of the 21st Century; PS21, a non-national, nonpartisan, nonideological think tank in London, New York, and Washington. Before that, he spent twelve years as a reporter for Reuters covering defense, political risk, and emerging markets. Since 2016, he has been a member of the British Army Reserve and the UK Labour Party.

Bernard Avishai is a visiting professor of government at Dartmouth College and an adjunct professor of business at the Hebrew University of Jerusalem. A Guggenheim fellow, he is the author of dozens of articles on politics, business, and the Middle East Conflict. His latest book on Israel, *The Hebrew Republic,* was published in 2008. *Promiscuous: Portnoy's Complaint and Our Doomed Pursuit of Happiness* was published in 2012.

Satyen K. Bordoloi is a screenwriter, independent journalist, and documentary filmmaker based in Mumbai. He writes on cinema, Indian politics, and social issues and documents grassroots movement for justice in the nation on his YouTube channel YouTube .com/SatyenBordoloi.

Bryan Borzykowski is a Toronto-based business journalist. He's written for CNBC, BBC Capital, *Forbes, New York Times,* CNNMoney, *Canadian Business* magazine, and the *Globe and Mail.* He's also written three personal finance books and appears regularly on Canada's CTV News Channel.

David Cole (co-editor) is the National Legal Director of the American Civil Liberties Union, the Hon. George J. Mitchell Professor in Law and Public Policy at Georgetown Law, a frequent contributor to the *New York Review of Books* and *The Nation,* and the author of *No Equal Justice, Enemy Aliens, Engines of Liberty,* and several other books. He lives in Washington, D.C.

Nic Dawes is deputy executive director for media at Human Rights Watch. He was previously Chief Content Officer at India's *Hindustan Times* and editor in chief at South Africa's leading political and investigative newspaper, the *Mail & Guardian.* As chairperson of the South African National Editors' Forum he has been an activist for press freedom and freedom of information in his home country, working to forestall regulatory and legislative efforts to curtail media independence.

Carlos de la Torre is a professor of sociology and former director of international studies at the University of Kentucky. Born in Ecuador, he is the author of *Populist Seduction in Latin America* and editor of *The Promises and Perils of Populism: Global Perspectives.* He has published extensively on Latin American populism and on the sociology of racism in Latin America.

Ariel Dorfman is a Chilean-American author whose plays (among them *Death and the Maiden*) have been performed in over one hundred countries and whose numerous writings (novels, stories, poems, essays) have been translated and published in more than sixty languages. Accompanied by his wife, Angélica, Ariel divides his time between Chile and the United States, where he is professor emeritus of literature at Duke University. A regular contributor to the most important newspapers worldwide, his most recent book is the memoir *Feeding on Dreams*.

Miklós Haraszti is a Hungarian author and professor, a fellow at the Center for Media, Data, and Society of the Central European University's School of Public Policy, and director of research on human rights at the CEU Center for European Neighborhood Studies. He was a founder of Hungary's human rights and free press movement in the 1970s and a member of Parliament in the 1990s.

N. Turkuler Isiksel is a political scientist from Turkey and the James P. Shenton Assistant Professor of the Core Curriculum at the Department of Political Science at Columbia University. Isiksel's research focuses on the ways in which descriptive and normative categories tailored to the nation-state apply to institutions that wield political power beyond that context. She is the author of *Europe's Functional Constitution: A Theory of Constitutionalism Beyond the State* (Oxford, 2016).

Melik Kaylan has worked as a journalist based mostly in New York for twenty-five years. He has written about ancient places, war zones, political upheavals and far frontiers for the *Wall Street Journal*, *Newsweek*, *Politico*, and *Forbes* covering an area from the China–North

Korea border to the Caucasus, Iraq, Iran, Syria, Turkey, and Eastern Europe.

Mohamed Keita is a freelance writer and former Africa advocacy coordinator of the Committee to Protect Journalists. Born in Mali, raised in Dakar, Senegal, and New York City, and living in Evanston, Illinois, Keita has written a number of essays which have appeared in publications including *The New York Times, The Christian Science Monitor, The Huffington Post, TheHill.com, Attacks on the Press, Africa Review, True Africa, Africa Is a Country,* and *Of Note.* He is a member of the World Policy Institute's Program for African Thought. Follow him on twitter @ModKeita.

Alexey Kovalev is a Russian journalist and media critic. He worked for Russian state news agency RIA Novosti and is the founder and editor of noodleremover.news, a fact-checking website.

Suketu Mehta is an associate professor of journalism at New York University and award-winning author of *Maximum City: Bombay Lost and Found.* Mehta's work has been published in *The New Yorker, The New York Times Magazine, National Geographic, Granta, Harper's Magazine, Time,* and *Newsweek* and has been featured on NPR's *Fresh Air* and *All Things Considered.* Mehta was born in Calcutta and raised in Bombay and New York.

Nick Robinson is a lecturer in political science at Yale University and a Schell Visiting Human Rights Fellow at Yale Law School. Previously, Nick spent seven years in South Asia, clerking for the chief justice of the Indian Supreme Court, working at Human Rights Law Network in New Delhi, and teaching at National Law School–Bangalore, Lahore University Management Sciences, and Jindal Global Law School. He was also a senior fellow at the Centre for Policy Research in New Delhi.

Tim Rogers is *Fusion*'s senior editor for Latin America. He was a foreign correspondent in Central America for a decade, reporting for a dozen US publications. Tim was a Nieman Fellow at Harvard in 2014.

Andrés Miguel Rondón is an economist living in Madrid. He's a Venezuelan citizen and grew up there. He also lived for six years in Wales and Scotland.

Jim Rutenberg is Media Columnist and former political correspondent for *The New York Times*.

George Soros has been a prominent international supporter of democratic ideals and causes for more than thirty years. His philanthropic organization the Open Society Foundations, supports democracy and human rights in more than one hundred countries.

Alexander Stille is an award-winning author and journalist. He has worked as a contributor to *The New York Times, La Repubblica, The New Yorker,* and *The New York Review of Books,* among other publications. He is the author, among other books, of *The Sack of Rome: Media + Money + Celebrity = Power = Silvio Berlusconi*. He has lived in Milan and Rome and in New York City, and is the San Paolo Professor of International Journalism at Columbia.

Melanie Wachtell Stinnett (co-editor) is a Boston-based writer and former director of policy and communications at the Tobin Project. She has previously published on regulatory policy and Supreme Court litigation trends and is the coauthor (with Senator Sheldon Whitehouse) of *Captured: The Corporate Infiltration of American Democracy* (The New Press).

Margaret Sullivan is the media columnist for *The Washington Post*. Before joining the *Post*, she was *The New York Times*' public editor, and previously the chief editor of *The Buffalo News*. She was a member of the Pulitzer Prize Board from 2011 to 2012, and was twice elected as a director of the American Society of Newspaper Editors, where she led the First Amendment committee. Sullivan has also taught in the graduate schools of journalism at Columbia University and City University of New York.

Nadezhda (Nadya) Tolokonnikova is an artist, political activist, and founding member of Pussy Riot, the punk rock art collective that garnered international headlines and support after several members were sent to jail following a performance in the Moscow Cathedral of Christ the Saviour. Tolokonnikova is the recipient of the Lennon Ono Grant for Peace and is a co-recipient of the Hannah Arendt Prize for Political Thought. Following her release in 2013, she opened the Mordovia office of Zona Prava, a prisoners rights nongovernmental organization. Later, she started MediaZona, an independent news service now partnered with *The Guardian*.

Alberto Barrera Tyszka is a Venezuelan poet, novelist, and television screenwriter. Formerly a professor of literature at Central University of Venezuela, he is coauthor of the internationally bestselling and critically acclaimed biography *Hugo Chávez: The Definitive Biography of Venezuela's Controversial President* and the author of the novel *The Sickness*. This essay was translated by Carolina Grooscors from the Spanish.

Paul Waldman is a weekly columnist and senior writer for *The American Prospect*. He also writes for the Plum Line blog at *The Washington Post* and *The Week*. His writing has appeared in dozens of newspapers, magazines, and websites, and he is the author or co-author of four books on media and politics.

Ai Weiwei (b. 1957) is an artist who resides and works in both Berlin and Beijing. His father, the poet Ai Qing, was denounced by

China's Communist Party in 1958 and his family was sent to labor camps, first near the North Korean border and then eventually in Xinjiang province. They returned to Beijing in 1976 after the end of the Cultural Revolution. Ai studied animation at the Beijing Film Academy, then studied art in New York in the early 1980s. Upon returning to China a decade later, Ai advocated for experimental artists by publishing underground books and curating avant-garde exhibitions. He has worked in many media, including sculpture, installation, photography, architecture, and film. He is an outspoken advocate of human rights and freedom of speech. He is the recipient of the Václav Havel Prize in Creative Dissent in 2012 and the Amnesty International Ambassador of Conscience Award in 2015.

Luigi Zingales, a professor of entrepreneurship and finance at the Booth School of Business at the University of Chicago, is the author of *A Capitalism for the People: Recapturing the Lost Genius of American Prosperity.* Zingales currently directs the Stigler Center, aimed at promoting and disseminating research on regulatory capture, crony capitalism, and the various distortions that special interest groups impose on capitalism. He also blogs on https://promarket.org/.

Celebrating 25 Years
of Independent Publishing

Thank you for reading this book published by The New Press. The New Press is a nonprofit, public interest publisher celebrating its twenty-fifth anniversary in 2017. New Press books and authors play a crucial role in sparking conversations about the key political and social issues of our day.

We hope you enjoyed this book and that you will stay in touch with The New Press. Here are a few ways to stay up to date with our books, events, and the issues we cover:

- Sign up at www.thenewpress.com/subscribe to receive updates on New Press authors and issues and to be notified about local events
- Like us on Facebook: www.facebook.com/newpressbooks
- Follow us on Twitter: www.twitter.com/thenewpress

Please consider buying New Press books for yourself; for friends and family; and to donate to schools, libraries, community centers, prison libraries, and other organizations involved with the issues our authors write about.

The New Press is a 501(c)(3) nonprofit organization. You can also support our work with a tax-deductible gift by visiting www.thenewpress.com/donate.